HOLIDAY

PLAYS BY PHILIP BARRY

HOLIDAY
A Comedy in Three Acts

BY

PHILIP BARRY

SAMUEL FRENCH
Thos. R. Edwards   Managing Director
NEW YORK   LOS ANGELES

SAMUEL FRENCH Ltd.   LONDON
1929

First printing March, 1929
Second printing April, 1929
Third printing December, 1929
Fourth printing October, 1930

MANUFACTURED IN THE UNITED STATES OF AMERICA
BY THE VAIL-BALLOU PRESS, INC., BINGHAMTON, N. Y.

TO HOPE WILLIAMS

"Holiday" was first produced by Arthur Hopkins at the Plymouth Theatre in New York City on November 26, 1928. It was directed by Arthur Hopkins and the settings were designed by Robert Edmond Jones.

CHARACTERS

Edward Seton
Ned Seton
Julia Seton
Linda Seton
Johnny Case
Seton Cram
Laura Cram
Nick Potter
Susan Potter
Henry
Charles
Delia

Action and Scene

ACT I

A Room on the Third Floor of Edward Seton's house in New York, December, this year.

ACT II

A Room on the Top Floor of Edward Seton's House, New Year's Eve, this year.

ACT III

The Room on the Third Floor, twelve days later.

ACT ONE

ACT ONE

Scene: A room on the third floor of EDWARD SETON'S
*house in New York. The only entrance is at Left. It is
a very large rectangular room of the Stanford White
period. The panelling is heavy, the mouldings are
heavy, the three long windows looking out over the
park at Back, are hung with heavy curtains. The
portrait of* SETON'S *father, by a contemporary English
master, hangs over the fireplace, at the right. It is a
handsome room, and quite a comfortable room, but
rich, very rich. At Right and Left are two comfortable
sofas, a table behind each. On one table are two tele-
phones, one for the house, the second for outside. On
the other table, magazines and newspapers, and a
cigarette-box. This side of the sofa, near Center,
are two upholstered benches and at Right and Left of
each, a large chair. In the corners of the room, at
Back, stand two more chairs, a table and lamp beside
each.*

*Time: It is about twelve o'clock on a bright, cold
Sunday morning in mid-December, this year.*

*At Rise: A fire is burning in the fireplace. Sunday
papers are strewn upon a low table and beside a chair
near it.*

JULIA SETON *is seated at a desk, Right, writing a
note. She is twenty-eight, and quite beautiful. She
writes in silence for a few minutes, then calls, in re-
sponse to a knock at the door:*

JULIA

Yes? (HENRY *enters from Left.* HENRY *is the butler. He is fifty, of pleasant appearance, of pleasant manner.*) Oh, hello, Henry. How have you been? [*She seals the note.*

HENRY

Well, thank you, Miss. We're very glad to have you back again.

JULIA

It was a lovely trip.

HENRY

—A Mr. Case to see you, Miss. He said you expected him, so Charles is bringing him up.

JULIA

That's right. How many are we for lunch?

HENRY

Six I believe. Only Mr. and Mrs. Cram are expected.

JULIA

Hasn't Miss Linda friends, too?

HENRY

Not as we've been told, Miss.

JULIA

Have an extra place set, will you?

HENRY

Yes, Miss.

[HENRY *collects the newspapers from the floor and chairs, and piles them in a neat pile upon a table. After a moment* CHARLES, *a younger man-servant, appears in the doorway.*

CHARLES

Mr. Case, Miss.

[JULIA *rises from the desk and calls in the direction of the hall:*

JULIA

Come in, Johnny! Quick!—Of all slow people!

[CHARLES *stands aside to admit* JOHNNY CASE, *and enters after him.* JOHNNY *is thirty, medium-tall, slight, attractive-looking, luckily not quite handsome. He goes at once to* JULIA.

JOHNNY

There was a traffic-jam. Men were dying like flies.—Did you really go to church?

JULIA

Yes, but I ducked the sermon. I was sure you'd get here before me. You're staying for lunch, you know.

JOHNNY

Thanks, I'd love to. (*Both look warily at the two men tidying up the room.*)—I'm actually hungry again. Those same old shooting-pains.

JULIA

Isn't it extraordinary the appetite that place gives you? You should have seen the breakfast I ate on the train.

JOHNNY

Why wouldn't you join me? You were invited.

JULIA

Miss Talcott would have swooned away. She's the world's worriedest chaperon as it is. (HENRY *goes out.* CHARLES *has begun to gather ash-trays upon a larger tray.*) —You can leave the trays till later, Charles.

CHARLES

Very well, Miss.
[*He moves toward the door.* JULIA *talks against his exit.*

JULIA (*to* JOHNNY)

Have you ever known such cold?

JOHNNY

Never.

JULIA

It's hard to believe it was twenty degrees lower at Placid.

JOHNNY

You don't feel it, there.

JULIA

That's what they say.—And you can close the door, Charles. It makes a draught.

CHARLES

Yes, Miss.

JULIA

When Mr. Seton comes in, would you ring this room from the door? Two short ones.

CHARLES

Very good, Miss.
[*He goes out, closing the door after him. For a moment* JULIA *and* JOHNNY *stand transfixed looking at each other. Then* JULIA *smiles slightly and says:*

JULIA

Hello, Sweet— (*In an instant* JOHNNY *is beside her and she is in his arms, being kissed. At length she stands off from him, murmuring:*) Johnny—Johnny—mind your manners.

JOHNNY

But dear, where are we?

JULIA

We're here, all right.
[JOHNNY *moves away from her and looks about him.*

JOHNNY

But where's "here"?

JULIA

Where I live. Don't you like it?

JOHNNY

But Julia, seriously, what *is* all this?

JULIA

All what?

JOHNNY

All this house—and armies of men underfoot picking up newspapers, and—

JULIA

Aren't you silly, Johnny. I told you where I lived. (*She seats herself upon a sofa.*) —I wrote it on the back of an envelope for you.

JOHNNY

But it's enormous. I'm overcome. It's the Grand Central. How can you stand it?

JULIA

I seem to manage.

JOHNNY

Don't you find you rattle around a good deal in it?

JULIA

I hadn't noticed that I did.
[JOHNNY *cups his hands and calls through them.*

JOHNNY

Hoo! (*then:*) There's a bad echo.

JULIA

You stop criticizing this house, or I'll call the bouncer.

JOHNNY

But you must all be so *rich,* Julia!

JULIA

Well, we aren't poor.

JOHNNY

You should have told me, you really should.

JULIA

Would it have made any difference?
[JOHNNY *laughs.*

JOHNNY

Lord, yes! I'd have asked you to marry me in two days, instead of ten.
[*A pause. Then:*

JULIA

How do you mean?

JOHNNY

I went through an awful struggle. You've no idea. I had very definite plans for the next few years, and at first a wife looked like quite a complication.

JULIA

What were the plans?

JOHNNY

For one thing, I was worried about having enough for both of us. If I'd known, I'd have spared myself. It's simply swell now. Good Julia.

JULIA

Aren't you funny, Johnny.

JOHNNY

Why?

JULIA

To talk about it.

JOHNNY

It? Money? Why? Is it so sacred?

JULIA

Of course not. But—

JOHNNY

I'm simply delighted, that's all.

JULIA

—That I have—uh—money?

JOHNNY

Yes. Sure.
[*She laughs.*

JULIA

You're amazing.

JOHNNY

But why not?—If I'd suddenly discovered you could play the piano I'd be delighted, wouldn't I?

JULIA

Is it like knowing how to play the piano?

JOHNNY

Well, they're both very pleasant accomplishments in a girl.

JULIA

But, my dear, you're going to make millions, yourself!

JOHNNY

Oh no I'm not.

JULIA

You are too!

JOHNNY

—Am not.

JULIA

Are too.
[*A brief pause.*

JOHNNY

How did you happen to decide I'd do, Julia?

JULIA

I fell in love with you, silly.

JOHNNY

You might have done that, and still not have wanted to marry me.

JULIA

I do, though.

JOHNNY

You know awfully little about me.

JULIA

I know enough.—You aren't trying to get out of anything are you, Johnny?

JOHNNY

Watch me.

JULIA

Because you haven't a chance, you know.
[*She rises and goes to the window at Back.*

JOHNNY

But what's there different about me? What did it?

JULIA

You're utterly, utterly different.

JOHNNY

—I am a man of the pee-pul—

JULIA

That might be one reason.

JOHNNY

I began life with these two bare hands.

JULIA

—So did the gentleman over the fireplace. (JOHNNY *looks at the portrait above the mantel.*) —Take heart from Grandfather.

JOHNNY

You wouldn't tell me you're *those* Setons!

JULIA

Forgive us, Johnny, but we are.
[JOHNNY, *overwhelmed, lowers his head.*

JOHNNY

It's too much.

JULIA (*lightly*)

—What man has done, man can do—or words to that effect.
[*She is looking out the window, down into the street.*

JOHNNY

See here, child—if you think I'm a budding young Captain of Industry, or—

JULIA

Sh—wait a minute.

JOHNNY

What's the matter?

JULIA

It's the motor. At least I think—yes, it is.

JOHNNY

Him?

JULIA

Wait a minute—No—it's only Linda. Father must have decided to walk home with Ned.

JOHNNY

Did you tell him, as you planned to?
[JULIA *again moves toward the sofa.*

JULIA

Father? Just exactly as I planned to.

JOHNNY

I'm still not sure that church was a good place.

JULIA

I wanted to give him a chance to think, before he started talking. He never talks in church.

JOHNNY

What did you say?

JULIA

I said, "Look here, Father: I'm going to marry Johnny Case." And he said "What's that?" And I said: "I said, I'm going to marry Johnny Case."

JOHNNY

And he never even peeped?

JULIA

Oh yes.—"And who may Johnny Chase be?" "Case," I said, "Not Chase." "Well, Case, then?"—I told him I'd met you at Placid, that he'd meet you at luncheon and that you were with Sloan, Hobson, Hunt and Sloan.—That was right, wasn't it?

JOHNNY

—Sloan, Hobson, *Hunter* and Sloan.

JULIA

It was near enough. He said, "I know Sam Hobson," and began to pray rapidly—and that was all there was to it.

JOHNNY

But probably there'll be more.

JULIA

Yes, probably a lot more—I hope you're feeling strong.
[*They seat themselves together upon the sofa at Right.*

JOHNNY

Seriously, how do you think he'll take it?
[JULIA *laughs.*

JULIA

—Seriously! (*Then:*) You'll have one big thing in your favor, Johnny.

JOHNNY

What?

JULIA

You'll see.

JOHNNY

I know: It's this necktie.

JULIA

Johnny—

JOHNNY

Julia—

JULIA

Don't jest, boy.

JOHNNY

Oh darling, let's not let the fun go out of it!

JULIA

Is it likely to?

JOHNNY

No, but—

JULIA

Say it.

JOHNNY

What was the point of spilling it so quickly?

JULIA

I had to tell Father. It would be different if Mother were alive. I could have broken it gently through her, I suppose. But as it is—

JOHNNY

—Eventually, I know. But why the rush?

JULIA

I had to tell him. He'd never have forgiven me.

JOHNNY

It could have been such a swell guilty secret for awhile.

JULIA

I can't see what particular fun a secret would have been.

JOHNNY

Can't you, dear?

JULIA

No.

JOHNNY

All right.

JULIA

Oh don't say "all right" that way! You don't mean "all right."

JOHNNY (*smiles*)
All right.

JULIA

You're the most outspoken, direct man I've ever known, and you sit there, sobbing over—

JOHNNY

It's all right, dear. Really it is.

JULIA

I thought you wanted us to be married as soon as possible.

JOHNNY

I do.

JULIA

Well, then.

JOHNNY

When shall we?

JULIA

There's another place Father comes in.

JOHNNY

I should think it would be pretty much up to you.

JULIA

You don't know Father.

JOHNNY

But let's not have an elaborate one—wedding, I mean.

JULIA

I doubt if we can avoid it. We've got to think of Father.

JOHNNY

It's getting pretty complicated.

JULIA

You didn't think it would be simple, did you?

JOHNNY

I suppose I just didn't think.

JULIA

You couldn't have. (*In sudden exasperation.*) Oh Johnny, *Johnny*—what's the matter with you?

JOHNNY

I just hate the thought of sitting down with a man and being practical about you—so soon, I mean.
[JULIA *softens.*

JULIA

—Angel. (*She kisses him, lightly.*) It's got to be done, though.

JOHNNY

All right. I'll gird up my loins.—You know, I'll bet he'll hate this necktie. It doesn't look substantial.

JULIA

You might sit like this—covering it with your hand.

JOHNNY

I love you, Julia.

JULIA

I love you, Johnny.

JOHNNY

That's the main thing, isn't it?

JULIA

Darling, that's everything—

JOHNNY

Kiss?

JULIA

With pleasure—
[*They kiss.*

JOHNNY

—Don't go.

JULIA

I wouldn't think of it.

JOHNNY

It'd be swell to have this whole day free with no
ordeals to face.

JULIA

It'll be over soon.—I think we'll have Ned and
Linda on our side.

JOHNNY

Lord, do they have to mix in, too?

JULIA

Well, they're my brother and sister.

JOHNNY

Are they good guys?

JULIA

—Dears. Ned's a little inclined to drink too much, but I think he'll outgrow it. You ought to be able to help him, I think. Linda's a curious girl. She's developed the queerest—I don't know—attitude toward life. I can't make her out. She doesn't think as we do at all, any more.

JOHNNY

We?

JULIA

—The family. Father's worried sick about her. I think *we* can help her a lot though—I hope we can. [JOHNNY *rises and goes to the fireplace.*

JOHNNY

She might prefer to work it out for herself. So might Ned.

JULIA

You *are* strange this morning, Johnny.

JOHNNY

How?

JULIA

You seem—not to like things quite as much as you might.

JOHNNY

Oh yes I do!

JULIA

We can't just wander forever up snowy mountains through pine woods with never a care, you know.

JOHNNY

Come here, darling. (*He goes to her, she to him. They meet.*) —We can do better than that.

JULIA

Do you suppose?

JOHNNY

I know.
[JULIA'S *head drops.*

JULIA

Oh, I feel so awfully sad all at once.

JOHNNY

Don't—*don't.* Don't ever— (*His grasp tightens upon her shoulders.*) Look up here—! (*With an effort, she looks up.*) —Now please kiss me several times.
[*She kisses him, once, twice, lightly.*

JULIA

Is that all right?

JOHNNY

All right, hell. It's perfect.
[*He bends to kiss her again, when the door suddenly opens and* LINDA SETON *enters, in hat and fur coat.* LINDA *is twenty-seven, and looks about twenty-two. She is slim, rather boyish, exceedingly fresh. She is smart, she is pretty, but beside* JULIA'S *grace,* JULIA'S *beauty, she seems a trifle gauche, and almost plain. She is pulling off her hat.*

LINDA

I must say, that of all the boring— (*She stops at the sight of* JULIA *and* JOHNNY.) Why, Julia. For shame, Julia. (JULIA *and* JOHNNY *part.* LINDA *throws her hat and gloves upon a chair.*) Is this a way to spend Sunday morning? Who's your partner? Anyone I know?

JULIA

It's— (*She recovers her composure.*) —This is Mr. Case—my sister Linda.

JOHNNY

How do you do?

LINDA

Well, thanks.—And you?

JOHNNY

I couldn't be better.

LINDA

Good.

JULIA (*with dignity*)

—*Johnny* Case, his name is. I'm going to marry him.

LINDA

That makes it all right then. (*She takes off her coat.*) Who's coming to lunch? Susan and Nick didn't telephone, did they?

JULIA

—In just about one month I'm going to marry him.

LINDA

Stand over here in the light, will you, Case? (JOHNNY *turns to her scrutiny.*) —But I've never even seen you before.

JULIA

Neither had I, until ten days ago at Placid.

LINDA (*to* JOHNNY, *with hope*)

You aren't a guide, are you?

JOHNNY

No. I'm a lawyer.

LINDA

Wouldn't you know it.

[JULIA *seats herself upon a chair at Right.*

JULIA

I want you to be maid-of-honor, Linda.

LINDA

I accept. What'll we wear? (*She sits upon the bench at Left, and* JOHNNY *upon the sofa facing her.*) Listen: is this what came over Father in church?

JULIA

I imagine so.

LINDA

Then you've told him already.

JULIA

Yes.

LINDA

Tsch-tsch, this modern generation. (*To* JOHNNY:) Well, young man, I hope you realize what you're getting in for.

[DELIA, *a housemaid of about thirty-five, comes in, takes* LINDA'S *coat, hat and gloves, and goes out with them.*

JULIA

That's pleasant.

LINDA

I don't mean you. You're divine. I mean Father—
and Cousin Seton Cram and Laura and the rest of
the outlying Setons—and the general atmosphere of
plenty, with the top riveted down on the cornu-
copia—

JULIA

Johnny will try to bear up, won't you, Johnny?

JOHNNY

I'll do my best.

[LINDA *goes to* JULIA *and seats herself upon the
bench facing her.*

LINDA

But how *did* you happen to get together? Tell Linda
everything.

JULIA

Well, I was walking along the road with Miss Talcott one morning on the way to the rink and who
should I see but—

LINDA

—*Whom* should I see but—

JULIA

—And who should I see but this man coming along,
carrying skis.

LINDA

Fancy that. A downright romance. Go on, dear—

JULIA

Do you really want to know?

LINDA

I'm hungry for romance, sister. If you knew the way my little heart is beating against its bars right this minute.

JULIA

He had a very queer look on his face.

LINDA

I can believe that. His eyes must have been burning.

JULIA

As a matter of fact, the trouble was with his nose. So I stopped him and said: "I suppose you don't realize it, but your nose is frozen." And he said: "Thanks, I hadn't realized it." And I said: "Well it is." And he said: "I don't suppose there's anything you personally could do about it."

LINDA

Fresh.

JULIA

I thought so too.

JOHNNY

She was fresh to mention it. It looked to me like an out-and-out pick-up.

LINDA

Obviously.

JULIA

I know a good thing when I see it.

LINDA (*to* JOHNNY)

—So you swept her off her snowshoes?

JOHNNY

It was touch-and-go with us.

LINDA (*to* JULIA)

I think I like this man.

JULIA

I was sure you would.

LINDA

Well my dears, take your happiness while you may.

JOHNNY

Watch us.
[JULIA *laughs.*

JULIA

No—*don't* watch us! Hello, Ned—
[NED SETON *enters from the hall. He is twenty-six. He is as handsome in his way as* JULIA *is in hers. His features are fine, a little too fine. He displaces very little, but no one minds: he is a nice boy.* JOHNNY *rises.* NED *goes to* JULIA.

NED

Oh, *you're* back.—Then it was you who took that shaker out of my room.

JULIA

This is Mr. Case—my brother Ned.
[JOHNNY *moves to* NED. *They shake hands briefly.*

NED

How do you do?—It was you who took it, Julia, and I'm getting sick of your meddling in my affairs.

JULIA

I'm going to marry him.

[NED *turns slowly, as* JULIA's *words penetrate, and regards* JOHNNY.

NED

You've got a familiar look about you.

JOHNNY

That's good.

NED

Is your name Johnny Case?

JOHNNY

Johnny Case.

NED

—One Saturday, quite a while ago, I went down to New Haven for a game. Afterwards, you took me all the way home from the Field, and put me to bed somewhere.

LINDA

How sweet.

JOHNNY

Call me Nana.

[*He goes to the sofa at Right.*

NED

I never got a chance to thank you. Thanks.

JOHNNY

It's all right.—Any time.

[NED *settles down with a newspaper on the sofa at Left.*

NED

He's a good man, this Case fellow.

LINDA

The point is, there's no moss apparent, nor yet the slightest touch of decay.

NED

I expect Father'll be a job. When do they come to grips?

JULIA

Before luncheon, I suppose.

[LINDA *rises.*

LINDA

That soon? See here, Case, *I* think you need some coaching.

JOHNNY

I'd be grateful for anything in this trouble.

LINDA

Have you anything at all but your winning way to your credit?

JOHNNY

Not a thing.

JULIA

Oh hasn't he though!

LINDA

The first thing Father will want to know is, how are you fixed?

JOHNNY

Fixed?

LINDA (*firmly*)

—Fixed.—Are you a man of means, and if so, how much?

JULIA

Linda!

LINDA

Be still, Beauty. (*To* JOHNNY.) I know you wouldn't expect that of a man in Father's position, but the fact is, money is our god here.

JULIA

Linda, I'll—! —Johnny, it isn't true at all.
[NED *looks up from his paper.*

NED

No?—What is, then?

LINDA

Well, young man?
[JOHNNY *goes to her.*

JOHNNY

I have in my pocket now, thirty-four dollars, and a package of Lucky Strikes. Will you have one?

LINDA

Thanks. (*She takes a cigarette from him.*) —But no gilt-edged securities? No rolling woodlands?

JOHNNY

I've got a few shares of common stock tucked away in a warm place.

LINDA

—Common? Don't say the word. (*She accepts a light from him.*) I'm afraid it won't do, Julia.—He's a comely boy, but probably just another of the vast army of clock-watchers.
[*She moves toward the window.* JOHNNY *laughs and seats himself on the sofa at Right.*

NED (*from behind his newspaper*)

How are you socially?

JOHNNY

Nothing there, either.

LINDA (*turning*)

You mean to say your mother wasn't even a Whoozis?

JOHNNY

Not even that.

JULIA

Linda, I do wish you'd shut up.

NED

Maybe he's got a judge somewhere in the family.

LINDA

Yes, that might help. Old Judge Case's boy. White
pillars. Guitars a-strummin'. Evenin', Massa.

NED

You must know some prominent people. Drop a few
names.

LINDA

—Just casually, you know: "When I was to Mrs.
Onderdonk's cock-fight last Tuesday, whom should
I see but Mrs. Marble. Well, sir, I thought we'd die
laughing—"

JULIA (*to* JOHNNY)

This is a lot of rot, you know.

JOHNNY

I'm having a grand time.

LINDA

" 'Johnny,' she says to me—she calls me 'Johnny'—"

JULIA

Oh, will you be *quiet!* What on earth has set you off
this time?

LINDA

But it's dreadful, sister. (*To* JOHNNY.) —Just what
do you think you're going to prove with Edward
Seton, financier and cotillion-leader?

JOHNNY

Well, I'll tell you: when I find myself in a position

like this, I ask myself: What would General Motors do? Then I do the opposite.

[LINDA *laughs and reseats herself.*

LINDA (*to* JULIA)

It'll be a pity, if it doesn't come off. It'll be a real pity.

JULIA

It will come off. (*To* JOHNNY.) Father isn't at all as they say he is.

JOHNNY

No?

JULIA

Not in the least.—Ned, where is he? Didn't he come in with you?

JOHNNY

Don't hurry him. There's no hurry.

NED

He said he had to stop to see Sam Hobson about something.

JULIA (*to* JOHNNY)

You.

JOHNNY

That's nice. I hope I get a good character.

LINDA

If it does go through all right, are you really going to make it quick?

JULIA

The second week in January. The tenth.

LINDA

—Announcing when?

JULIA

Right away—next Saturday say.

LINDA (*eagerly*)

Oh darling, let me give a party for it!

JULIA (*puzzled*)

Do you want to? I thought you hated the thought
of—

LINDA

I want to! Not Father. *I* want to.

JULIA

Why of course, dear. We'd love it.

NED

Who'd like a drink?
[*No one bothers with him.*

LINDA

—Father's to have nothing to do with it. And we
won't send out cards. I'll telephone people.—Saturday's New Year's Eve, do you know it? Oh Lord,
Lord—let's have some fun in this house before you
leave it!

JULIA

Why, Linda—

LINDA

I mean it! Let me, won't you?

JULIA

If Father doesn't mind.

LINDA

No ifs, at all!—And just a few people—very few.
Not a single bank of pink roses and no String Quar-
tet during supper. All I want by way of entertainment, is just one good tap-dancer. Let me plan it.
Let me give it. Julia, let *me* do something for you
once—*me*, Julia.

JULIA

I'd love it, dear. I really would.

LINDA

It won't be a ball, it'll be a simple sit-down supper—
and you know where?—The old playroom.

JULIA

Why not the—

LINDA

—Because the playroom's the one room in this house
anyone's ever had fun in!

NED

I haven't been up there for ten years.

LINDA

That's your loss, Neddy. I've installed a new fangled
gramophone, and I sit and play to myself by the
hour. Come up sometime. It's worth the trip. (*She*

turns suddenly to JOHNNY.) —Do you know any living people, Case? That's a cry from the heart.

JOHNNY

One or two.

LINDA

Give me a list. (*To* JULIA.) —Seton and Laura can't have a look-in—is that understood? (*To* JOHNNY.) —A terrible cousin and his wife—the Seton Crams. They're coming for lunch today. I hope your digestion's good. (*To* JULIA.) —Not a look-in, remember.

JULIA

I don't know how you'll keep them out.
[LINDA *rises abruptly.*

LINDA

Oh Julia—this is important to me!—No one must touch my party but me, do you hear?

JULIA

All right, darling.

LINDA

If anyone does, I won't come to it.

NED

—At that, you might have a better time. (*He rises.*) Look here, Case—

JOHNNY

Yes?

NED

Cocktails aren't allowed at mid-day, so just before

luncheon's announced I'll ask you if you care to
brush up.

JOHNNY

And guess what I'll say.

JULIA

There'll be wine with lunch, Ned.

NED

You have to give it something to build on, don't you?
[*A buzzer sounds twice.* JULIA *and* JOHNNY *rise.*

JULIA

—It's Father! He's home.

LINDA

He'll go up to his sitting-room first.
[JULIA *moves toward the door.*

JULIA

I know. Come on with me, Ned.

NED

I don't want to see him.

JULIA

Please come with me. (NED *goes out. She turns to*
JOHNNY.) You wait here with Linda a moment. I'll
either come down again or send word. Just talk
awhile.
[*She follows* NED *out. A brief pause. Then* LINDA
goes to the bench at Left, and JOHNNY *to the one at*
Right.

LINDA

However do you do, Mr. Case?

JOHNNY

—And you, Miss—uh—?

LINDA

Seton is the name.

JOHNNY

Not one of the bank Setons!

LINDA

The same.

JOHNNY

Fancy!—I hear a shipment of ear-marked gold is due in on Monday.
[*Now they are seated.*

LINDA (*in her most social manner*)

Have you been to the Opera much lately?

JOHNNY

Only in fits and starts, I'm afraid.

LINDA

But, my dear, we must do *something* for them! They entertained us in Rome.

JOHNNY

—And you *really* saw Mount Everest?

LINDA

Chit.

JOHNNY

Chat.

LINDA

Chit-chat.

JOHNNY

Chit-chat.

LINDA

Will that go, for the preliminaries?

JOHNNY

It's all right with me.

LINDA

I love my sister Julia more than anything else in this world.

JOHNNY

I don't blame you. So do I.

LINDA

She's so sweet, you don't know.

JOHNNY

Yes, I do.

LINDA

She's beautiful.

JOHNNY

She's all of that.

LINDA

—And exciting, too—don't you think?

JOHNNY

—Don't. I'll start gittering.

LINDA

It's terribly important that she should marry the right person.

JOHNNY

That's important for everyone.

LINDA

It's particularly so for Julia.—I suppose you realize you're a rather strange bird in these parts.

JOHNNY

How's that?

LINDA

You don't know the kind of men we see as a rule.— Where have you been?

JOHNNY

Oh—working hard.

LINDA

Nights?

JOHNNY

Nights too.

LINDA

What about these little jaunts to Placid? Come clean, Case.

JOHNNY

That's the first holiday I've ever had.

LINDA (*unconvinced*)

Yes.

JOHNNY

You heard what I said.

LINDA

Then you can't have been working long.

JOHNNY

Just since I was ten.
[*She frowns, puzzled.*

LINDA

—Ten. At what?

JOHNNY

—Anything I could get. Law, the last few years.

LINDA

—Must be ambitious.
[JOHNNY *expels his breath in a long, tired jet.*

JOHNNY

I am. Not for that, though.

LINDA

For what, then?

JOHNNY

Oh—to live. Do you mind?
[*There is a pause.*

LINDA

What is it you've been doing?

JOHNNY

I don't call what I've been doing, living.

LINDA

No?
[*He shakes his head.*

JOHNNY

—Awhile ago you asked me if I knew any living people. I know damn few.

LINDA

There aren't but damn few.

JOHNNY

Well, I mean to be one of them some day. Johnny's dream.

LINDA

So do I. Linda's longing.

JOHNNY

There's a pair called Nick and Susan Potter—

LINDA

So you know Nick and Susan?

JOHNNY

I should say I do.

LINDA

So that's where I've heard your name. Aren't they grand?

JOHNNY

It seems to me they know just about everything. Maybe I'm wrong.

LINDA

You're not, though.

JOHNNY

Life must be swell, when you have some idea of what goes on, the way they do.

LINDA

They get more fun out of nothing than anyone I know.

JOHNNY

You don't have such a bad time yourself, do you?

LINDA (*leaning forward*)

Case, are you drawing me out?
[JOHNNY *laughs*.

JOHNNY

Sure! Come on!

LINDA

Well, compared to the time I have, the last man in a chain-gang thoroughly enjoys himself.

JOHNNY

But how does that happen?

LINDA

You tell me, and I'll give you a rosy red apple.

JOHNNY

It seems to me you've got everything.

LINDA

Oh it does, does it?

JOHNNY

What's the matter? Are you fed up?

LINDA

—To the neck.—Now tell me about *your* operation.

JOHNNY

I had been ailing for years—I don't know—life seemed to have lost its savor—

LINDA

Couldn't you do your housework?

JOHNNY

Every time I ran upstairs, I got all run-down. (LINDA *laughs.* JOHNNY *leans forward:*) You'd better come on a party with Julia and me.

LINDA

Anytime you need an extra girl, give me a ring.— When?

JOHNNY

How's Tuesday?

LINDA

Splendid, thanks.—And how's Thursday?

JOHNNY

Blooming.

LINDA (*reflectively*)

—Looked badly the last time we met.

JOHNNY

—Just nerves, nothing but nerves.
[*A moment's pause. Then:*

LINDA

—Do I seem to you to complain a good deal?

JOHNNY

I hadn't noticed it.

LINDA

Then I can let myself go a little: this is a hell of a life, Case.
[JOHNNY *looks about him.*

JOHNNY

What do you mean? All this luxe? All this—?

LINDA

You took the words right out of my mouth.

JOHNNY

Well, for that matter, so's mine.

LINDA

What's the answer?

JOHNNY

Maybe you need some time off, too—I mean from what you're doing, day in, day out—

LINDA

Days out, please—*years* out—

JOHNNY

All right: take it. Take the time—

LINDA

—And of course *that's* so easy.

JOHNNY

—It can be done. *I* intend to do it. I intend to take quite a lot of it—when I'm not so busy just making the wherewithal.

LINDA

Case, you astonish me. I thought you were a Willing Worker.

JOHNNY

I am, if I can get what I'm working for.

LINDA

And what would that be?

JOHNNY

Mine is a simple story: I just want to save part of my life for myself. There's a catch to it, though. It's got to be part of the young part.

LINDA

You'll never get on and up that way.

JOHNNY

All right, but I want *my* time while I'm young. And let me tell you, the minute I get hold of just about twenty nice round thousands, I'm going to knock off for as long as they last, and—

LINDA

Quit?

JOHNNY

Quit. Retire young, and work old. That's what I want to do.

LINDA

—Grand. Does Julia know about it?

JOHNNY

No—there's no use getting her hopes up until it happens.—Don't tell her, will you?

LINDA

She has enough of her own for two right now—or ten, for that matter. Mother and Grandfather did us pretty pretty.

[JOHNNY *shakes his head.*

JOHNNY

Thanks, but I've got to do myself—only just pretty enough.

LINDA

I see. That's foolish—but you're all right, Case. You haven't been bitten with it yet—you haven't been caught by it.

JOHNNY

By what?

LINDA (*so reverently*)

The reverence for riches.

[JOHNNY *laughs.*

JOHNNY

You *are* a funny girl.

LINDA

—Funny, am I? And what about you, you big stiff?
[JOHNNY *laughs, and rises.*

JOHNNY

—Just take Johnny's hand, and come into the Light,
sister. (JULIA *enters.* JOHNNY *turns to her.*) Did
you see him?

JULIA

I saw him.

LINDA

Julia! How was he?

JULIA

I don't know yet.—Johnny, you go up to Ned's room.
You haven't arrived yet. Take the elevator—
Father's coming down the stairs. Quick, will you?

JOHNNY

When do I arrive?

JULIA

One o'clock. It's quarter to.

JOHNNY

This is getting a little complicated, if you ask me.

JULIA

Nobody asked you. Go on! Do as you're told.
[JOHNNY *turns.*

JOHNNY

See here, you saucy—
[LINDA *goes to the fireplace.*

LINDA

Go on, Case. Don't expect simplicity here—just think of our Fifth Avenue frontage. (JOHNNY *laughs and goes out.* LINDA *turns to* JULIA.) Tell me: was Father awful?

JULIA

—The same old story, of course: I'm being married for my money.

LINDA

That's always flattering.—But Case didn't know our foul secret, did he?

JULIA

No.

LINDA

Even if he had, what of it?—And what good's all this jack we've got, anyway—unless to get us a superior type of husband?

JULIA

I hate you to talk like that! I hate it!

LINDA

Listen to me, Julia: I'm sore all the way through. I've been sore for a long time now, ever since I really saw how it—oh, never mind. Anyway, I don't doubt that if Case *had* known he'd still be running. You're in luck there.

JULIA

You do like him, don't you?

LINDA

She asks me if I like him!—My dear girl, do you realize that *life* walked into this house this morning? Marry him quick. Don't let him get away. And if Father starts the usual—where *is* Big Business, anyhow?

JULIA

He said he'd be right down.

LINDA

Stand your ground, Julia. If you don't know your own mind by now, you haven't got a mind. Name your date and stick to it. I'm telling you.

JULIA (*slowly*)

I want Father to see that Johnny has the selfsame qualities Grandfather had,—and that there's no reason why he shouldn't arrive just where he did.

LINDA

—If he wants to.

JULIA

—Wants to! You don't know Johnny. You don't know how far he's come already—and from what—

LINDA

—Or where he's going.

JULIA

I do! *I* know! I can see it clear as day! (*A moment. Then:*) Linda—

LINDA

What?

JULIA

It'll be awful to leave you.

LINDA

I don't know exactly what I'll do, when you go. I've got to do something—get out—quit on it—change somehow, or I'll go mad. I could curl up and die right now.

JULIA (*touched*)

Why, darling—

LINDA

Why, my foot. I don't look sick, do I? (*She moves to the fireplace.*) Oh, Lord, if I could only get *warm* in this barn! (*She crouches before the fire and holds her hands to it.*) —Never mind about me. I'll be all right. Look out for yourself. When Big Business comes down, just watch you don't let him— (*The door opens. She looks over her shoulder and sees her Father.*) —But by a strange coincidence, here he is now.

JULIA

Did you see Mr. Hobson, Father?
[EDWARD SETON *enters. He is fifty-eight, large, nervous, distinguished. He wears a black morning-coat, a white carnation in the buttonhole, and gray striped trousers. He takes nose-glasses from his nose and folds them away in a silver case.*

EDWARD

Yes.—Of course, my dear, there is another thing to be considered: What is the young man's background?

Is he the sort of person that—? Ah, good morning,
Linda.

LINDA

You saw me in church, Father. What's on your mind?
You look worried.

EDWARD

I presume Julia has told you her story?

LINDA

Story? She's told me the facts.

EDWARD

But we mustn't rush into things, must we?
(*A glance passes between* JULIA *and* LINDA. JULIA
goes to him.)

JULIA

I want to be married on January tenth, Father.
That's—that's just two weeks from Tuesday.
[EDWARD *moves to the table behind the sofa at Right,
and begins to search through the newspapers.*

EDWARD

Quite impossible.

LINDA

Why?

JULIA

Yes, why? I—I'm sure I couldn't stand a long engagement.

EDWARD

As yet, there is no engagement to stand.

LINDA

The boy has loads of charm, Father.

EDWARD (*quickly*)

> You know him?

LINDA

> I've heard tell of him.
> [EDWARD *tastes the word:*

EDWARD

> Charm.

LINDA

> —I suppose it's solid merit you're after. Well, the rumor is he's got that, too. Sterling chap, on the whole. A catch in fact.
> [NED *wanders in and seats himself upon the sofa at Left, with a newspaper.*

JULIA

> What did Mr. Hobson say, Father?

EDWARD

> We must find out about the young man's background.

JULIA

> What did he say?

EDWARD

> Have you the financial section of the Times, Ned?

NED

> No, I try to take Sundays off, when I can.

EDWARD

> —Which reminds me: I should like you to make a practice of remaining in the office until six o'clock.

NED

Six!—What for?

EDWARD

As an example to the other men.

NED

But there's nothing for me to do after three.

EDWARD

You will find something.

NED

Look here, Father—if you think I'm going to fake
a lot of—

EDWARD

Did you understand me, Ned?
[*A moment:* NED *loses.*

NED

—Oh, all right.

JULIA

What did Mr. Hobson say about Johnny, Father?
[EDWARD *settles himself upon the sofa with the finan-
cial section, now happily found.*

EDWARD

His report was not at all unfavorable.

LINDA

That must have been a blow.

JULIA

—But what did he *say?*

EDWARD

We must find out more about the young man, Julia. He seems to have some business ability—he has put through what looks like a successful reorganization of Seaboard Utilities. He holds some of the stock.

NED

Seaboard! Poor fellow—

EDWARD

—Shrewd fellow, perhaps. Hobson says signs are not unfavorable for Seaboard.—We'll buy some in the morning, Ned.

LINDA

Just another ill wind blowing money to Da-Da.

EDWARD

But we *must* know more about Mr. Chase's background.

LINDA

Case, Father, Case.

LINDA

Let it go. Chase has such a sweet banking-sound.

JULIA

He's from Baltimore.

LINDA

Fine old pre-war stock, I imagine.

NED

Wasn't there a Judge Case somewhere?

EDWARD

We shall see. We shall take steps to—

LINDA

Father, if you reach for a Social Register, I'll cry out with pain.

EDWARD (*with decision*)

Well, I most certainly intend to know more about the young man than his name and his birthplace.— He does not, of course, realize that you have spoken to me, as yet?

NED

Of course not.

LINDA

Julia works fast, but not *that* fast, do you Julia? [JULIA *does not answer.*

EDWARD

I propose not to allow the subject of an engagement to come up in my first talk with him. I believe I am competent to direct the conversation.—You and Ned, Julia, may excuse yourselves on one pretext or another. I should like you to stay, Linda.

LINDA

I *knew* I should have learned shorthand. [EDWARD *smiles.* HENRY *enters.*

EDWARD

I shall trust your memory.—Yes, Henry?

HENRY

Mr. Case wishes to be announced, sir.

EDWARD

Yes.

[HENRY *goes out, closing the door after him.* EDWARD *arranges his cuffs, and takes a firmer seat in his chair.*

LINDA

—So does Mr. Case's engagement. I want to give a party for it New Year's Eve, Father.

JULIA

Wait a minute, dear—

EDWARD (*watching the doorway*)

You may give a party if you like, Linda, but whether to announce an engagement, we shall see—

LINDA

—Another point about my party is that it's *my* party—mine.

EDWARD

Yes?

LINDA

Yes—and as such, I'd like to run it. I can do quite well without your secretary this time, darling—and without Seton's and Laura's helpful hints, I can do brilliantly.—There's someone at the door.

NED

Keep a stiff upper lip, Father. No doubt the fellow is an impostor.

[EDWARD *laughs.*

EDWARD

Oh, we shall learn many things this morning! He is
not the first young man to be interviewed by me.

JULIA

Father—

EDWARD

Yes, daughter?

JULIA

Remember: I know what I want. (JOHNNY *enters*.)
Oh, here you are!

JOHNNY

Here I am.

JULIA

Father, this is—Mr. Case.
[JOHNNY *goes to* EDWARD. *They shake hands.* NED
rises.

EDWARD

How do you do, Mr. Case?

JOHNNY

How do you do, sir?

EDWARD

—My daughter, Linda.

LINDA

How do you do?

JOHNNY

How do you do?

EDWARD

> And my son, Ned.

JOHNNY

> How do you do?

NED

> I recall your face, but your figure puzzles me.

EDWARD

> Julia, if you and Ned will do the telephoning I spoke
> of, Linda and I will try to entertain Mr. Case until
> the others come—won't we, Linda?

LINDA

> Sure. I'm game.
> [JULIA *moves toward the door.*

JULIA

> —Coming, Ned?

NED (*following her*)

> I wonder what we'd do without the telephone.
> [*They go out.*

EDWARD

> Sit down, Mr. Case!

JOHNNY

> Thank you.
> [*He seats himself upon the bench, Left, and* LINDA
> *upon a small stool at the fireplace.*

EDWARD

> I presume, like all young people, you have the bad
> habit of smoking before luncheon?

JOHNNY

I'm afraid I have.

EDWARD

—A cigar?

JOHNNY

Not right now, thank you.
[EDWARD *lets himself down into a sofa.*

EDWARD

We've been quite at the mercy of the snow these days, haven't we?

JOHNNY

It doesn't seem much after Placid.

EDWARD

Placid—ah yes! My daughter Julia has just come from there.

JOHNNY

I know.
[*A brief pause. Then:*

EDWARD

—You are in business in New York, Mr. Case?

JOHNNY

Yes, I'm in the Law. I'm with Sloan, Hobson.

EDWARD

An excellent firm.—And a born New Yorker?

JOHNNY

No. I was born in Baltimore.—In 1897. July sixth.
I'm thirty.

EDWARD

Baltimore—I used to have many friends in Baltimore.—The Whites—the Clarence Whites—possibly you knew them.

JOHNNY

No, I don't believe I ever did.

EDWARD

—And then there was Archie Fuller's family—

JOHNNY

I'm afraid not.

EDWARD

—And let me see now—Colonel Evans—old Philip Evans—

JOHNNY

Nope. (*There is a silence. Then:*) I haven't been there in some years. And I shouldn't be likely to know them, anyway. My mother and father died when I was quite young. My father had a small grocery store in Baltimore, which he was never able to make a go of. He left a number of debts which my mother worked very hard to clear up. I was the only child, and I wasn't in a position to help very much. She died the May before my sixteenth birthday.
[LINDA *is listening with growing interest.*

EDWARD

But how sad.

JOHNNY

It *was* pretty sad.—I hadn't any connections, except for an uncle who's in the roofing business in Wilming-

ton. He wasn't much good though—he was inclined
to get drunk—still is—

LINDA

We have an uncle like that, but he keeps off roofs.
[JOHNNY *smiles at her, and continues:*

JOHNNY

—But I was what's called a bright boy, and I man-
aged to wangle a couple of scholarships. They helped
a good deal in school and college, and there were always plenty of ways to make up the difference. In
term-time I usually ran eating-joints and typed lec-
ture notes. In the summers I sold aluminum pots-
and-pans—

EDWARD (*weakly*)

Linda! Are you there, Linda?

LINDA

Yes, Father.

JOHNNY

—Or worked in a factory or on a newspaper. Once I
got myself engaged as a tutor. That was pretty un-
pleasant. Then there were department-stores at
Christmas and florists at Easter. During law school
I slept all night on a couch in a doctor's office, and
got fifteen a week for it. That was soft.

EDWARD (*it is all he can say*)

Admirable!

JOHNNY

No—it simply happened to be the only way to get
through. (*A brief pause. Then:*) Anything else, sir?

EDWARD

I beg your pardon?
[LINDA *rises.*

LINDA

I should think you would.

JOHNNY

—Is there anything more I can tell you about myself?

EDWARD

Why, uh—that is to say, uh—
[*He flounders, and stops. A moment, then* JOHNNY *moves toward him.*

JOHNNY

Well, Mr. Seton, how about it?

EDWARD

About it? About what?

JOHNNY

Julia and me.

EDWARD

You and Julia? I'm afraid I—

JOHNNY

—About our getting married.
[*There is a silence. Then:*

EDWARD

This is a complete surprise, Mr. Case. I don't know quite what to say to you.
[JOHNNY *smiles.*

JOHNNY

"Yes" would be pleasant.

EDWARD

I am sure it would. However, we must go into it rather more carefully, I am afraid.

JOHNNY

The only difficulty is the time. Julia's idea is January tenth. It's mine, too.

EDWARD

We shall see about that.

JOHNNY

May I ask *how* we shall see sir?

EDWARD

Mr. Case, I do not know you at all.

JOHNNY

I'll give you every opportunity you permit me. How's lunch to-morrow?

EDWARD

To-morrow I have several—

JOHNNY

—Tuesday?
[EDWARD *hesitates.*

EDWARD

Will you meet me at the Bankers' Club at one on Friday?

JOHNNY

I'm terribly sorry, but Friday's out. I've got to go

to Boston on business.—Better make it to-morrow.
[*A moment.* NED *and* JULIA *re-enter. Then* EDWARD
speaks, hastily:

EDWARD

—Very well, I shall arrange my appointments.—
Ah Ned, Julia—and what do you suppose can be
keeping the Crams?
[*But* JOHNNY *cuts in before they can reply:*

JOHNNY

—Thank you. In the meantime, I think Mr. Hobson
or Mr. Sloan might say a good word for me. I'm nobody at all, as things go. But I'm quite decent and
fairly civilized, and I love your daughter very much
—which isn't a bit hard. She seems to like me quite a
lot too, and that's about all that can be said for me
—except that I think we've a simply grand chance
to be awfully happy.—What do *you* say, Julia?

JULIA

Oh, so do I!

LINDA

Come on, Father, be an angel. *I* think he's a very
good number.

EDWARD

I am afraid it is too important a matter to be decided off-hand.

JULIA

But I want to be married on the—

EDWARD (*with sudden sharpness*)

You will be married, Julia, when I have reached a favorable decision—and upon a day which I will name.

JULIA

I—our plan was—the tenth, and sail that night on—

EDWARD

The tenth is out of the question.

JULIA

Oh but Father—! I—

EDWARD

—And we shall let it rest at that, for the moment.

LINDA

But you'll come round, Father! I have a swell hunch you'll come round. Oh Lordy, Lordy, what fun! Let's all join hands and—

[*Voices are heard from the hall.*

EDWARD

Seton?—Laura?—Is that you I hear?

LINDA

You bet it is.—Let's *not* join hands.

[SETON CRAM *and his wife,* LAURA, *enter.* SETON *is thirty-six, somewhat bald, inclined to a waistline, but well turned-out in a morning-coat, striped trousers and spats.* LAURA *is thirty-two, a shade taller than* SETON, *with a rather handsome, rather disagreeable face. She is as smartly dressed as a poor figure will allow.*

SETON

　Hello, hello!

EDWARD

　—How are you, young man?

SETON

　Blooming, thanks. We walked all the way up.
　[*They shake hands with* EDWARD.

LAURA

　I do hope we're not late, Uncle Ned.

EDWARD

　No indeed!

LINDA

　You're early.

LAURA

　Julia, my dear, you're back. (*She kisses her and then
　bears down upon* LINDA.) —And Linda! How simply
　stunning!
　[LINDA *wards off the impending kiss.*

LINDA

　Careful, Laura—I've got the most terrible cold.

LAURA (*returning*)

　But I never saw you looking better!—Hello Ned.

NED

　Hello.

EDWARD

　This is—uh—Mr. Case—my nephew, Mr. Cram,
　and Mrs. Cram.
　[LAURA *inclines her head.*

SETON

How do you do?

JOHNNY

How do you do?

[NED *edges away from* LAURA. EDWARD, *still stunned, stares in front of himself.*

LAURA

—Isn't it horrid how chapped one's hands get this weather? I don't know *what* to do. How was Placid, Julia?—You must have had *such* a divine time. Were there loads of amusing people there?—And lots of beaux, too—oh you needn't deny it!—We know Julia, don't we, Seton?—And you Linda—we haven't seen *you* for ages—(*She seats herself upon the bench at Right.*) —Now sit right down and tell us *everything* you've been doing—

LINDA

Well, take the average day: I get up about eight-thirty, bathe, dress, and have my coffee.—Aren't you going to brush up before lunch, Ned?

NED

—Would you care to brush up before lunch, Case?

JOHNNY

I think I shall, if I may.

[*He follows* NED *to the door.*

LINDA

—Julia?

JULIA

I'm all right, thanks.

LINDA

But look at *me*, will you! (*She moves quickly across the room after* NED *and* JOHNNY, *flecking imaginary dust from her dress as she goes.*) —Simply *covered* with dust!—Wait, boys!

CURTAIN

ACT TWO

Scene: The Playroom on the top floor is a long and spacious low-ceilinged room with white wood-work and pale blue walls upon which are lightly-traced story-book designs in silver, white and green.

At Right and Left there are two windows with window seats below them, curtained in a white-starred cretonne of a deeper blue than the walls.

The only entrance is from the hall at Back.

At Right, there is a low platform for horizontal-bars and a punching-bag, above which, a pair of trapezes swing from the ceiling. At present they are tied up. Against the back wall behind them is a glass cabinet containing a collection of old toys, arranged on shelves in orderly rows.

Also at Right is a table, with tablecloth spread, and four small chairs. Against the back wall at Left is an old-fashioned music-box, and in the corner near it a small electric gramophone. Also at Left is a low couch and a table, a miniature easy-chair and a folding-cushion.

Time: New Year's Eve, this year.

At Rise: The Playroom is empty, and lit only by a pale night-glow from the windows. A moment, then JULIA *opens the door, and calls:*

JULIA

Linda! (*There is no answer. Dance music is heard from downstairs.*) She isn't here.

[NED *reaches past her to an electric button and lights the room.*

NED

I didn't say she was. All I said was it's where she comes, as a rule, when she finds herself in a jam.
[*They come into the room. Both are in evening clothes. In one hand,* NED *carries two whisky-and-sodas. He puts one glass on the table and retains the other.*

JULIA

I don't believe she's in the house.
[NED *takes a swallow of his drink.*

NED

Maybe not.

JULIA

I told them all at dinner that she had a blinding head-ache, but expected to come down later.

NED

That's as good as anything— (*And another swallow.*) Let's get out of here. This room gives me a funny feeling.

JULIA

Wait a minute.— You know how furious Father was when she wasn't there for dinner— (*She goes and shuts the door, closing out the music.*) What can we do, Ned?

NED

Search me.
[*She moves to a chair and seats herself.*

JULIA

But it's her party!

NED

Don't make me laugh, Julia. It was, maybe, until you and Father took it over.

JULIA

I did?

NED

You stood by and saw it done. Then the Crams got hold of it. Among you, you asked the whole list— which was just what Linda didn't want. You threw out the team of dancers she'd engaged for supper, and got in that troupe of Scotch Songbirds. You let Farley, with his Flower Fancies, turn it into a house of mourning. Among you, you made Linda's funny little bust into a first-class funeral. I can't say I blame her, no. However— (*He raises his glass.*) —drink to Linda.

JULIA

Well I do! She should have realized that Father couldn't announce my engagement without *some* fuss.

NED

She should have, yes. But unlike me, Linda always hopes. (*Again his glass is raised.*) Bottoms up to Linda.

JULIA

Don't Ned.

NED

Don't what?

JULIA

You've been drinking steadily since eight o'clock.
[NED *goes to the table near the couch.*

NED

Yes?— Funny old Ned. On New Year's Eve, too.
[*He drains his glass and takes up the other.*

JULIA

Will you kindly stop it!

NED

Darling sister, I shall drink as much as I like at any
party I agree to attend. (*She turns from him with
an exclamation.*) —And as much as I like, is as much
as I can hold. It's my protection against your tire-
some friends. Linda's out of luck, she hasn't one.
[JOHNNY *comes in. Music and voices are heard from
downstairs.*

JOHNNY

—Believe it or not, I've been talking politics with
an Admiral. (*He looks about him.*) —What a nice
room!

NED

It's too full of ghosts, for me. It gives me the creeps.

JULIA

She isn't here, Johnny.

JOHNNY

Linda?

JULIA

Yes, of course.

JOHNNY

Did you expect she would be?

JULIA

Ned thought so.

NED

Ned was wrong.
[HENRY *and* CHARLES *enter.* HENRY *carries table-linen
and silver and a tray of plates and glasses;* CHARLES
*a pail of ice containing two bottles of champagne,
and a plate of sandwiches. They go to the table.*

JULIA

Isn't there room for everyone downstairs, Henry?

HENRY

Miss Linda telephoned to serve supper here for six
at half-past eleven, Miss.

NED

Ned was right.

JULIA

From where did she telephone, do you know?

HENRY

She didn't say, Miss.
[*There is a pause.* HENRY *and* CHARLES *proceed to set
the table.*

JOHNNY (*to* JULIA)

I think I know where she is, if that's any help.

JULIA

You? Where—?

JOHNNY

With Nick and Susan Potter.

JULIA

What's she doing with them?

JOHNNY

Dining, I imagine.

NED

It's eleven-twenty now.

JULIA

Where did you get your information, Johnny?

JOHNNY

I met her coming in this afternoon. She said she wouldn't stay in the house to-night. Apparently it meant more to her than anyone thought.

NED

Not than I thought. I warned Father.

JOHNNY

It was no use talking to her. She was going out to dine somewhere by herself. I knew that Nick and Susan were having Pete Jessup and Mary Hedges, so I telephoned Susan and asked her to ask Linda, too.

JULIA

I wish you had spoken to me first.

JOHNNY

Why?

JULIA

People like that aren't good for Linda.
[JOHNNY *looks at her for a moment, puzzled, and then laughs.*

JOHNNY

What are you talking about, Julia?

JULIA

They make her even more discontented than she is. Heavens knows why, but they do.

NED

Apparently she's bringing them back with her.
[HENRY *and* CHARLES *go out, closing the door after them.*

JULIA

Well, they certainly can't expect to have supper up here by themselves.

NED

No? Why not?

JULIA

They simply can't, that's all.

NED

What is this consipracy against Linda, anyway? Are you all afraid she might cause a good time here, for once—and if she did, the walls might fall down? Is that it?
[JULIA *does not reply.* JOHNNY *seats himself near her.*

JOHNNY

I do love this room, don't you, Julia?

JULIA (*briefly*)

Yes.—It was Mother's idea for us.

JOHNNY

She must have been sweet.

JULIA

She was.

NED

—Father wanted a big family, you know. So she had Julia straight off, to oblige him. But Julia was a girl, so she promptly had Linda. But Linda was a girl—it looked hopeless. (*His voice rises.*) —So the next year she had me, and there was much joy in the land. —It was a boy, and the fair name of Seton would flourish. (JULIA *looks at him in alarm.*) —It must have been a great consolation to Father. Drink to Mother, Johnny—she tried to be a Seton for awhile, then gave up and died.—Drink to Mother—

[JOHNNY *laughs uneasily.*

JOHNNY

You're talking through your hat, Ned.

NED

But I'm not.

JULIA (*to* JOHNNY)

Can't you possibly persuade him that he's had enough?

NED

It's all right, Julia: you heard what I said.—There's a bar in my room, if you want anything, Johnny. Tell as many of the men as you think need it. It's all very pleasant and hole-in-the-wall like everything else that's any relief in this house.—Drink to Father. [*He drains his glass, sets it down upon a table, turns on his heel and goes out, closing the door after him.*

JULIA

We must do something about them—we *must*, Johnny!

JOHNNY

—Him and Linda.

JULIA

Yes, yes!

JOHNNY

I don't see what.—It seems a lot more goes on inside them than we've any idea of. Linda must be at the end of some rope or other. As for Ned—

JULIA

He always does this—always—
[JOHNNY *rises.*

JOHNNY

He began sometime.—I'll keep an eye on him, though, and if he stops making sense I'll get him to bed somehow.

JULIA

—And Linda's got to bring her friends downstairs.— People know there's something wrong, now—they must know.—She's simply *got* to!

JOHNNY

All right, darling. Only—

JULIA

Only what—

JOHNNY

—Do try to enjoy to-night, won't you?

JULIA

But I am, Johnny. I think it's a lovely party!

JOHNNY

Then how about getting that frown from between your eyes and not feeling personally responsible for three hundred guests, and a brother and sister?

JULIA

—Someone's got to be.

JOHNNY

—Let your Father, then.

JULIA

Poor man. Reporters have been after him all day long.

JOHNNY

Me, too. I've never felt so important.

JULIA

I hope you didn't talk.

JOHNNY

I just asked for offers for the story of how I wooed and won you. Farm Boy Weds Heiress as Blizzard Grips City.

[JULIA *laughs.*

JULIA

What *did* you say?

JOHNNY

I didn't see them.

JULIA

That's right. Father was awfully anxious that nothing be added to what he sent in—except, of course, what they're bound to add themselves.

JOHNNY

Evidently it's a good deal.

JULIA

Well, that we can't help.

JOHNNY

The French Line wrote me. They want to give us a suite, in place of the cabin.

JULIA

I doubt if we ought to accept it.

JOHNNY

No? Why not?

JULIA

I think it might not look so well. I'll ask Father.
[*A brief pause. Then:*

JOHNNY

Perhaps we oughtn't to go abroad at all. Perhaps *that's* too great an evidence of wealth.

JULIA

Now Johnny—

JOHNNY

—But we're going, my dear, and in the most comfortable quarters they choose to provide.

JULIA

What a curious tone for you to take.
[*He looks at her in amazement, then laughs genuinely.*

JOHNNY

Julia, don't be ridiculous! "Tone to take." (*She turns from him.*) —We may be suddenly and unexpectedly important to the world, but I don't see that we're quite important enough to bend over backwards.
[*A silence. Then:*

JULIA

Of course, I'll do whatever you like about it.

JOHNNY

It would be nice if you'd like it too.
[*She returns to him.*

JULIA

And I'll like it too, Johnny.
[*He bends and kisses her, lightly.*

JOHNNY

—Sweet.— (*He takes her by the hand and draws her toward the door.*) —Come on, let's go below and break into a gavotte.
[JULIA *stops.*

JULIA

—Do something for me, will you?

JOHNNY

Sure.

JULIA

—Stay here till Linda arrives, then make her come down. I can't wait. *Some* female member of the household's got to be around, if it's only the cook.

JOHNNY

—I'll *ask* her to come down.

JULIA

Insist on it!

JOHNNY

Well, I'll do whatever a gent can in the circumstances.

JULIA

You're *so* irritating! Honestly, I hate the sight of you.

JOHNNY

Julia—

JULIA

What?

JOHNNY

Like hell you do.

JULIA

I know. It's hopeless. (*She goes to the door, opens*

it, then turns to him again. Laughter is heard from downstairs.) Do as you like—I love you very much.

JOHNNY

—You get through that door quick and close it after you, or you won't get out at all.

JULIA

—Just to look at you makes my spine feel like—feel like—
[*He moves swiftly toward her, but finds the door closed. He stands for a moment staring at it, transfixed, then pulls it open, calling "Darling!" —But instead of* JULIA, *he finds* NICK POTTER.

NICK

Hey! What is this?

JOHNNY

Nick!
[NICK *moves away from him, scowling, and straightening his coat. He is about thirty-four, with an attractive, amusing face.*

NICK

—Get fresh with me, and I'll knock your block off. (*He sees the champagne and goes to it.*) What have we here—some kind of a grape-beverage?

JOHNNY

Mumm's the word.—Where's Susan?

NICK

Coming.—I hear you're engaged. Many happy returns. Is it announced yet?

JOHNNY

Thanks.—No, it's to come with a roll of drums at midnight—"A lady has lost a diamond-and-platinum wrist-watch."

NICK

—With that gifted entertainer, Mr. Edward Seton, at the microphone—

JOHNNY

That's the plan.

NICK

I heard about his work with this party.—He has the true ashman's touch, that man.

JOHNNY

He's been all right to me.

NICK

Oh sure—he believes you're a comer. That's what won him over so quickly—the same stuff as Grandpa Seton himself—up-from-nothing—hew to the line— eat yeast. Me—of course I'm God's great social menace because I never got out and did Big Things.

JOHNNY

I really like him. I like him a lot.

NICK

Keep your men on him, though. Don't relax your vigilance.

[*He is opening the bottles and filling the glasses. Music and voices are heard through the open door.*

JOHNNY

—You think, for instance, that if *I* should quit business—

NICK

Just try it once. Why he'd come down on you like Grant took Bourbon.

JOHNNY

You've got him all wrong, Nick.

NICK

Maybe.—Anyhow, you're not really thinking of it are you?

[JOHNNY *goes to the couch.*

JOHNNY

I am, you know!

NICK

On what, may I ask?

JOHNNY

Well, I've got a nice little mess of common stock that's begun to move about two years before I thought it would. And if it goes where I think it will—

NICK

—Haven't you and Julia a pretty good life ahead as it is, Johnny?

JOHNNY

You and Susan have a better one.

NICK

Listen, baby—I don't think I'd try any enlightened

living stuff on this family. They wouldn't know what
you were talking about.

JOHNNY

Julia would.

NICK

—Might. But the old man's a terror, Johnny. Honestly—you don't *know*.

JOHNNY

Enough of your jibes, Potter. You answer to me for
your slurs on a Seton.
[NICK *moves toward him.*

NICK

—Seats on a Slurton—I want to get three seats on a
Slurton for Tuesday night. (—*And confronts him
with an empty bottle.*) Go on hit me, why don't
you? Just hit me. Take off your glasses— (*And returns to the table.*) —I was dragged against my
will to this function. And somehow I don't seem to
so well.

JOHNNY

What?

NICK

—Function.
[LINDA *and* SUSAN *enter.* SUSAN *is thirty, smart and
attractive. She goes straight to* JOHNNY *and kisses
him.*

SUSAN

Cheers from me, Johnny.

JOHNNY

Thanks, Susan.

SUSAN *and* NICK (*together*)

We only hope that you will be as happy as we have been.

[LINDA *closes the door. Voices and music cease to be heard.* NICK *continues to fill the glasses*

JOHNNY (*to* LINDA)

What did you do with Pete and Mary?

LINDA

They're coming in a heated barouche.

JOHNNY

Linda, I'm to inform you that there's another party going on in the house.

LINDA

You mean that low-class dance hall downstairs? (*She moves toward* NICK.) Don't speak of it.

[NICK *gives her a glass of wine, and then one to* SUSAN.

NICK

Here, Pearl, wet your pretty whistle with this.

[NICK *and* JOHNNY *take glasses.* SUSAN *raises hers.*

SUSAN

—To Johnny and his Julia.

JOHNNY

Julia—

[*They drink.* LINDA *seats herself in a chair near the table.*

SUSAN

—Merry Christmas, from Dan to Beersheba.

NICK (*examining the table*)

—Only sandwiches? What a house!

LINDA

There's solid food on the way.

NICK

I'll trade twenty marbles and a jack-knife for the carcass of one chicken, in good repair.

LINDA

You should have been with us, Johnny. Not one word of sense was spoken from eight to eleven.

SUSAN

—When Linda got homesick.

LINDA

I'm a die-hard about this evening and this room. I only hope nobody else wanders in.

[JOHNNY *seats himself near* LINDA.

NICK

I tell you who'd be fun.

LINDA

Who?

NICK

Seton and Laura.

LINDA

They wouldn't stay long.—You see those trapezes?

NICK

Yes?

LINDA

Time was when Seton and I used to swing from them
by our knees, and spit at each other.

NICK

Great!

LINDA

I'm happy to say now, I rarely missed.

JOHNNY

But aren't we going downstairs?

LINDA

No, Angel, we're not.

NICK

It's grand here. It takes sixty years off these old
shoulders. (*He looks at his watch.*) Eleven-forty.—
Doctor Stork's on the way, dears, with Little Baby
New Year.

[*He goes and seats himself with* JOHNNY *and* LINDA.

LINDA

I wish someone would tell me what *I'm* to do next
year—and the year after—and the year after that—

SUSAN

What you need is a husband, Linda.
[*She joins the group.*

LINDA

Have you got any addresses?

SUSAN

He'll arrive. I only hope you'll know how to act when he does.

LINDA

Well, I won't take No for an answer.

NICK

Don't you do it.

LINDA

And in the meanwhile what? Hot-foot it around the world with a maid and a dog? Lie on one beach after another getting brown?

NICK

Oo, I *love* to play in the sand.

SUSAN (*to* LINDA)

—You just won't stay put, will you, child?

LINDA

And grow up to be a committee-woman and sit on Boards? Excuse me Susan, but from now on any charity work *I* do will be for the rich. They need it more.

[NICK, SUSAN *and* JOHNNY *are eating sandwiches and sipping their wine.*

NICK

Now look, Linda—let me tell you about yourself, will you?

LINDA

Go ahead.

NICK

There's more of your grandfather in you than you think.

LINDA

Boo.

NICK

There is, though. He wasn't satisfied with the life he was born into, so he made one for himself. Now you don't like *his* five-story log cabin so you're out in the woods again with your own little hatchet.

SUSAN

The Little Pioneer, with Linda Seton.

JOHNNY

—Linda's off on the wrong foot, though. She's headed up the fun-alley. She thinks having fun is the whole answer to life.

LINDA

I do?

JOHNNY

You do.—Me—it's not just entertainment *I'm* after —oh no—I want all of it—inside, outside—smooth and rough—let 'er come!

NICK

You're right, too.—Life's a grand little ride, if you take it yourself.

JOHNNY

—And no good at all if someone else takes you on

it. Damn it, there's *no* life any good but the one you
make for yourself.

SUSAN (*a protest*)

Hey, hey—

JOHNNY

—Except yours and Nick's, maybe.

LINDA

But they *have* made theirs!—Haven't you, Susan?

SUSAN

About half-and-half, I should say. I don't know quite
what we'd do if we had to earn our own living.

NICK

Earn it.—Is it settled about the wedding, Johnny?

JOHNNY

The twelfth—a week from Friday.

LINDA

Why not the tenth?

JOHNNY

Your Father had a corporation meeting.—Ushers'
dinner on Monday, Nick.

NICK (*to* SUSAN)

Don't wait lunch for me Tuesday.

SUSAN

Just come as you are.—Oh, I gave a scream.

LINDA

What's the matter?

SUSAN (*to* JOHNNY)

—Then you've put off your sailing, too?

JOHNNY

We had to.

SUSAN

Don't tell me it's the *Paris* now?

JOHNNY

Yes. Why?

SUSAN

But we changed ours from the tenth to the *Paris* so as not to bump into your wedding trip!

NICK

Well, we'll change back again.

JOHNNY

Don't think of it. It'll be great fun.

LINDA

Guess what *I* did in a wild moment this morning—

NICK

What?

LINDA

—Had my passport renewed—and Ned's. I want to get him away.

SUSAN

You're sailing then too?—It's a field-day!

LINDA

No—not till a week or so after.

JOHNNY

Come along with us, Linda. It'd be grand. We'd own the boat.

LINDA

You'll have had plenty of family by then, little man. We'll join up later.

JOHNNY

How long do you plan to stay over, Nick?

NICK

Oh—June—August—September—like the dirty loafers we are.

LINDA

Loafers nothing!

JOHNNY

You've got the life, you two.

LINDA

Haven't they? (*To* SUSAN.) You know, you've always seemed to me the rightest, wisest, happiest people ever I've known.

SUSAN

Why Linda, thanks!

LINDA

You're my one real hope in the world.

JOHNNY

Mine, too.

SUSAN

Well, when we're with a pair like you—shall I say it, Nick?

NICK

Just let them look at us: Beam, darling—
[SUSAN *beams.*

SUSAN

—The Beaming Potters.

NICK

—In ten minutes of clean fun—

NICK *and* SUSAN (*together*)
We hope you'll like us!
[*Then:*

NICK

—And what about you, Johnny? How long will you and Julia be there?
[*A moment.* JOHNNY *smiles. Then:*

JOHNNY

Well—maybe indefinitely.

LINDA

How do you mean? Julia said March.

JOHNNY

Julia doesn't know yet.

LINDA

Johnny, what *is* this?!

JOHNNY

Well, some stock that I got at about eight was kind enough to touch fifteen to-day. And if a deal I think's going through does go through, it'll do twice that.

SUSAN (*puzzled*)

I must be dumb, but—

JOHNNY

Friends, there's a very fair chance I'll quit business next Saturday.

LINDA

Johnny!

NICK

For good?

JOHNNY

—For as long as it lasts.

SUSAN

As what lasts? Have you made some money?

JOHNNY

I think I shall have, by Saturday.

SUSAN

Good boy!

LINDA

Oh, very good boy!

NICK

—And Julia doesn't know your little plan?

JOHNNY

I haven't breathed a word of it to her. I wanted to be sure first. It all depends on what a Boston crowd called Bay State Power does about it. I'll know that Monday.

LINDA

They'll do it! I don't know what it is, but I know they'll do it! Oh, Lord, am I happy! (*A moment. Then:*) But, Johnny—

JOHNNY

What?

LINDA

I'm scared.

JOHNNY

Of what?

LINDA

Listen to me a moment: Father and Julia— (*She stops, as* SETON *and* LAURA *appear in the doorway, and exclaims in disgust:*) My God, it's Winnie-the-Pooh!
[JOHNNY *and* NICK *rise.* LAURA *gazes about her.*

LAURA

But isn't this lovely!

SETON

Well, well, so here you are!
[*He comes into the room.* LAURA *follows.*

NICK

So we are.

SETON

Hello, Nick.—Hello, Susan!

NICK

How are you?

LAURA (*to* SUSAN)

My dear what fun! We simply never meet any more.

SUSAN

—Just a pair of parallel lines, I expect.

LAURA

I must say you're a picture, Susan.
[SUSAN *rises and goes to the couch.*

SUSAN

—Madame is in a tin bed-jacket, by Hammacher-Schlemmer.

LAURA

May we sit down a minute?
[*She seats herself in* NICK's *chair.*

LINDA

Why not?

LAURA

I've never been up here. It's awfully pleasant.

LINDA

We like it.

NICK

Of course, it's rather far from the car-line—

SUSAN

And the water isn't all it might be—

NICK *and* SUSAN (*together*)

—But *we* like it!

JOHNNY

Don't change it, friends. It's the poor man's club.

LAURA

What on earth are you all talking about?
[LINDA *rises and goes to the table.*

LINDA

Oh, just banter—airy nothings—give and take—

NICK

It's our defense against the ashman's touch.

LAURA

I *love* the decorations.

LINDA

They *love* to be loved.

LAURA

I'm afraid I don't follow you. You're not all tight, are you?

LINDA

On the continent, dear, on the continent.

NICK

We have a very high boiling-point.
[SETON *leans over and plucks* JOHNNY'S *sleeve.*

SETON

You old fox, you.

JOHNNY

Yes? How's that?

SETON

Sam Hobson's downstairs. He's just been telling me about your little haul in Seaboard. You might have let your friends in on it.

JOHNNY

There's still time. Climb aboard if you like.

SETON

I have already.—Do you know there's an order in our office to buy sixty thousand shares for Ross, of Bay State Power, all the way up to thirty?

JOHNNY (*quickly*)

Are you sure of that?

SETON

I took the order myself.

JOHNNY

Then that cinches it.

SUSAN

Is it a real killing, Johnny?

JOHNNY

For me it is!

SETON (*impressively*)

—Just thirty or forty thousand, that's all.

SUSAN

—No odd cents?

LINDA

Johnny—Johnny—

NICK

Let this be a lesson to you, young man.

SETON

—Anyone mind if I talk a little business?—The im-

pression in our part of town is, it's you who put
Seaboard on the map.

JOHNNY

I wouldn't go so far as that.

SETON

Ross said so himself.—Look here: we'd damn well like
to have you with us, in Pritchard, Ames.

JOHNNY

Thanks, I've heard about that.

SETON

The Chief's told you already?

JOHNNY

I saw him this afternoon.

SETON (*to* NICK)

—To begin at twice what he gets now—and probably
a directorship in Seaboard, to boot.

NICK

Well, well—to boot, eh?

SETON (*to* JOHNNY)

I hope you said Yes.

JOHNNY

I told him I'd let him know.

SETON

Believe me, when I tell you the first fifty thousand is
the hardest.—It's plain sailing after that.

LINDA (*suddenly*)

Look out, Johnny!

SETON

　　—In two years we'll make your forty thousand,
eighty—in five, two hundred.
　　[NICK *edges over to* JOHNNY.

NICK

　　—Lend a fellow a dime for a cup of coffee, mister?
　　[JOHNNY *laughs.*

SETON

　　Well, how about it?

JOHNNY

　　I'll let him know.

SETON

　　You couldn't do better than to come with us—not
possibly.
　　[JOHNNY *rises and puts his glass on the table.*

JOHNNY

　　It's awfully nice of you, it really is.

LINDA

　　Look out, look *out!*

JOHNNY

　　Don't worry, Linda.

SETON

　　—Just let me give you a brief outline of the possi-
bilities—

LINDA

　　That will do for business to-night, Seton.

SETON

I just want to tell Johnny—

LINDA

It's enough, really.
[SETON *laughs, and rises.*

SETON

You're the hostess!—Then let's all go downstairs and celebrate, shall we?
[LAURA *rises.*

LAURA

Yes, let's.—It's such a wonderful party.

LINDA

I'm not going downstairs.

SETON

Oh come along, Linda—don't be foolish.

LAURA

Do come, dear. Your Father said to tell you he—

LINDA

Yes—I thought so.—But I'm not going downstairs.
[NICK *moves away from them to the other side of the room.*

NICK

Where's the old music-box we used to play, Linda?

LINDA

Over there—but I've got something better— (*She goes to the gramophone in the corner.*) Listen—it's electric—it'll melt your heart with its—

NICK

Take it away.
[SUSAN *rises.* SETON *and* LAURA *move toward the door.*

SUSAN

Nick—you wouldn't go whimsical on us!

NICK

Oh God, for the old scenes—the old times—

SETON

It's a quarter-to-twelve now, you know—
[NICK *is examining the music-box.*

NICK

Welcome, little New Year—

LAURA

Linda, I really think that—

LINDA

I know, Laura.
[NICK *reads the music-box's repertory from a card:*

NICK

"Sweet Marie" — "Fatal Wedding" — "Southern Roses"—

SUSAN

—And *this* is the way they used to dance when Grandmama was a girl.
[NICK *covers his eyes, and gulps.*

NICK

Don't. My old eyes can scarcely see for the tears.

LAURA

You're all absolutely mad.

[HENRY *and* CHARLES *enter, with a chafing-dish and a platter of cold meats. A chorus of male voices is heard from downstairs.*

SUSAN

Heavens, what would that be?

LINDA

It's the Scottish Singers, the little dears—
[*She is watching* JOHNNY.

NICK

I wouldn't have come, if I'd known the Campbells were coming—
[CHARLES *closes the door.* LINDA *starts a loud new dance-record on the gramophone.*

SETON (*angrily*)

What do you think this gets you, anyway?

LINDA

Peace and quiet!
[NICK *huddles himself in his arms.*

NICK

What a night! What a night!

SUSAN

What Nick really wants is some nice beer to cry into.

LINDA

Will everybody please stop sobbing! Stop it!—
Take some wine will you, Case?

JOHNNY

Thanks.

LINDA (*intensely*)

If you weaken now—!

JOHNNY

I never felt stronger.

[LINDA *turns to* SUSAN.

LINDA

Peter and Mary—they couldn't have ditched us, could they?

SUSAN

Oh, no, they'll be along—

NICK

Eleven forty-seven—what *can* be keeping old Doctor Stork?

[HENRY *and* CHARLES, *having placed the platter and chafing-dish upon the table, go out.*

LAURA (*at the door*)

Linda—really—people are beginning to wonder a little—

LINDA

I am *not going downstairs.*

[LAURA *laughs unpleasantly.*

LAURA

Well, of course if—

LINDA

But I wouldn't dream of keeping anyone who wants to—

[LAURA *stares a moment, then turns to* SETON.

LAURA

Apparently we aren't welcome here.

SETON

I gathered that some time ago.—Linda, I think your conduct toward your guests to-night is outrageous.

LAURA

And so do I.

LINDA

I imagined that was what brought you up, you sweet things.

SETON

If you ask me, it's one of the worst cases of down-right rudeness I've ever seen.

LINDA

And has someone asked you?

LAURA

—When a girl invites three hundred people to her house, and then proceeds to—

LINDA

I invited six people—three of whom you see before you. The others came on someone else's say-so—yours and Father's, I believe.

LAURA

Perhaps we'd better go home, Seton.

LINDA

Oh, you're here now. Stay, if you like. I'd prefer it, however, if you'd do your commenting on my be-

havior not to my face, but behind my back as usual—
[LAURA *opens the door.*

LAURA

Come, Seton—
[*She goes out, with all the hauteur she can command.*

SETON (*to* LINDA)

When I think of the—

LINDA

—Before you go, you wouldn't care to swing on the
old trapeze awhile, would you—? (*He stares. She
turns away.*) I suppose not. (SETON *goes out, closing
the door after him.* LINDA *moves toward the table.*)
Oh, the cheek, the cheek!

NICK

Someday they'll draw themselves up like that, and
won't be able to get down again. (*He goes to*
JOHNNY.) Well, Johnny—!

JOHNNY (*at the table*)

Lord, it's the grandest feeling—oh, wait till Julia
hears! On to-night, of all nights, too! What a break
that is!

LINDA

I've never been so happy for anyone in my life.

NICK

Go to it, boy!

JOHNNY

Oh, won't I? Watch me! (*Then:*) —Where'll we

spend the spring?—Let's all spend the spring together!

NICK

What do you say, Susan? Do you think we could stand them?

SUSAN

There'll always be a curse and a blow for you with us, Johnny.

LINDA

Can I come? Please, can I come, too—?
[*She trots in among them.*

NICK

Don't leave us, darling. We want you, we need you.
[SUSAN *joins them. She sits at the end of the table, opposite* NICK, *and* JOHNNY *and* LINDA *behind it, facing the front.* JOHNNY *refills the glasses and* SUSAN *and* LINDA *serve the food.*

SUSAN

How about the south of France?

JOHNNY

Why not?

LINDA

No, no—the air reeks of roses and the nightingales make the nights hideous.

JOHNNY (*overcome*)

Don't—don't—
[*He gives each of them a glass of wine.*

NICK (*a suggestion*)

If we went to Norway, we could all paint a house at midnight.

JOHNNY

—Norway's out. It's got to be some place you can swim all day long.—You know, it's just dawned on me that I've never swum enough. That's one of the things I want to do: *swim*.
[NICK *rises and leans upon the table.*

NICK

Young man, in the bright lexicon of youth there is no such word. Swimming is for idlers.

SUSAN

—And Hawaiians.

LINDA

—And fish.

NICK

Are you a fish? Answer me that.—Can you look yourself squarely in the eye and say "I am a fish"? No. You cannot.

JOHNNY

You are a hard man, sir.

NICK

It is life that has made me hard, son.

JOHNNY

—But I want only to be like you, Daddy—how can I be like you?

NICK

You ask me for the story of my success?—Well, I'll
tell you—

LINDA

Come—gather close, children.
[*They turn their chairs and face him.*

NICK

—I arrived in this country at the age of three
months, with nothing in my pockets but five cents
and an old hat-check. I had no friends, little or no
education, and sex to me was still the Great Mystery.
But when I came down the gang-plank of that little
sailing-vessel—steam was then unknown, except to
the very rich— Friends, can you picture that manly
little figure without a tug at your heart strings, and
a faint wave of nausea? But I just pulled my belt a
little tighter, and told myself "Don't forget you're a
Potter, Nick"—I called myself "Nick"—and so I
found myself at my first job, in the glass works. Glass
was in its infancy then—we had barely scratched the
surface—but I have never shirked work—and if there
was an errand to be run, I ran five errands. If someone wanted to get off at the third floor, I took him to
the tenth floor.—Then one day came my big chance.
I was in the glass-blowing department then—now
Miss Murphy's department—and a very capable little woman she is—

LINDA

Why, Mr. Potter, I'm no such thing.

NICK

Oh, yes you are, Miss Murphy! Well, sir, I was blowing glass like a two-year-old, whistling as I blew.
Suddenly I looked down and found in my hand—
a bottle—or what we now know as a bottle. I rushed
to my employer, a Mr. Grandgent, and said, "Look,
Mr. Grandgent—I think I've got something here."
Mr. Grandgent looked—and laughed—*laughed,* do
you understand?—I went from city to city like some
hunted thing, that laugh still in my ears. But with
me went my bottle. They called it Potters' Folly.
They said it would never work. Well, time has shown
how right they were. Now the bottle is in every home.
I have made the bottle a National Institution!—And
that, my dears, is how I met your grandmother.
[*He bows.* LINDA *rises, champagne-glass in hand.*

LINDA

—To one who, in the face of every difficulty, has
proved himself a Christian gentleman.—Music, music!
[*She goes to the gramophone and starts a record.*
SUSAN *rises.*

SUSAN

—To one who has been friend to rich and poor
alike—
[JOHNNY *rises.*

JOHNNY

—To one who, as soldier—

LINDA

—As statesman—

SUSAN

—As navigator—

JOHNNY

—As man about town—

LINDA

—As scout-leader—

NICK

—As Third Vice-President of the second largest spat-factory in East St. Louis—

JOHNNY

On behalf of the hook-and-ladder company of the First-Reformed Church, I want to say a few words about our brave Fire-Laddies. Has it occurred to you—?

[*The door opens and* JULIA *and* EDWARD *enter.*

EDWARD

Linda!

LINDA

Yes?

EDWARD

Please turn that machine off.

[SUSAN *goes to* NICK.

LINDA

You know Mr. and Mrs. Potter, Father—

EDWARD (*curtly*)

How do you do? (*Then, to* LINDA.) Turn it off, Linda—

[LINDA *stops the record.*

NICK (*to* SUSAN)

—Fell, or was pushed.

[JOHNNY *moves eagerly toward* JULIA.

JOHNNY

Julia! Listen darling! I've got a grand surprise for you—

EDWARD

Just a moment!—You must all come down, now. It's nearly twelve, and we want the entire party together to see the New Year in.

LINDA

But there are two parties, Father—the one down there and mine—*here*.

EDWARD

Please do as I say, Linda.

LINDA

I asked for permission to have a few of my friends in here to-night. You said I might. I've got some of them, now, and—

EDWARD

—I noticed you had.

LINDA

—And more are coming.

JULIA

They've come, haven't they?

LINDA

How do you mean?

JULIA

Peter Jessup and what's-her-name—Mary Hedges—

LINDA

What about them?

JULIA

They're downstairs.

LINDA

They—? —How long have they been there?

JULIA

Twenty minutes or so. I said you'd be down.

LINDA

Oh, you did, did you?

JULIA

—They're being very amusing. I said we expected them to be. Jessup has done his trained-seal act to perfection, and now I think Mary Hedges is about to give her imitations. (*There is a silence.* LINDA *stares at her, speechless.*) They're a great success, really.

LINDA (*without turning*)

Nick—will you and Susan bring them up to my sitting-room? I'll be there in a minute.

SUSAN

All right, Linda.
[*She moves toward the door.* NICK *follows, gazing anxiously at the ceiling as he goes.*

NICK

—The New Year ought to be just about passing over Stamford.

[*They go out, closing the door after them.* JOHNNY
goes to JULIA.

JOHNNY

Julia! Big news, dear—guess what's happened?

LINDA (*to* EDWARD *and* JULIA, *before* JULIA *can reply:*)
Oh, this is so humiliating.—Peter and Mary are my
guests, do you understand? Not paid entertainers—
[*She moves away from them.*

JULIA

I'm sorry. I simply couldn't imagine mixing-in people
like that to no purpose.

LINDA

Couldn't you?

JULIA

No.—But of course I can't follow your reasoning
these days, Linda. I can't follow it at all.

EDWARD (*to* LINDA)

There's no cause for temper, child. Just run along
now, and we'll follow. Julia and I want to talk to
Johnny for a moment.
[JULIA *turns again to* JOHNNY.

JULIA

What is it, Johnny? Quick, tell me!

LINDA

—Listen to me, Father: to-night means a good deal
to me—I don't know what, precisely—and I don't
know how. Something is trying to take it away from

me, and I can't let it go. I'll put in an appearance
downstairs, if you like. Then I want to bring a few
people up here—the few people in the world I can
talk to, and feel something for. And I want to sit
with them and have supper with them, and we won't
disturb anyone. That's all right with you, isn't it?

EDWARD

Your place is downstairs.

LINDA

Once more, Father: this is important to me. Don't
ask me why. I don't know. It has something to do
with—when I was a child here—and this room—and
good times in it—and—

EDWARD

What special virtue this room has, I'm sure I don't
see.

LINDA

You don't, do you—no—you can't. Well, I'll tell you
this room's my home. It's the only home I've got.
There's something here that I understand, and that
understands me. Maybe it's Mother.

EDWARD

Please do as I have told you, Linda.

LINDA

I suppose you know it's the end of us, then.

EDWARD

Don't talk nonsense. Do as I say.

LINDA

It *is* the end. But all the same, I'm going to have supper here to-night in my home with my friends.

EDWARD

I have told you—

LINDA

—You thought I'd come around, didn't you? You always think people will come around. Not me: not to-night. And I shan't be bothered here, either. Because if there's one thing you can't stand, it's a scene. I can promise you one, if you interfere. I can promise you a beauty.

[EDWARD *turns from her.* LINDA *looks about her, at the room.*

EDWARD

—Well, Johnny, so there's good news, is there?

LINDA (*suddenly*)

Was Mother a sweet soul, Father? Was she exciting?

EDWARD (*to* JOHNNY)

—A happy day all around, eh? An engagement to be announced, New Year's to celebrate—and now—

LINDA

Was Mother a sweet soul, Father? Was she exciting?

EDWARD

Your mother was a very beautiful and distinguished woman. (*To* JOHNNY.) Naturally, I am delighted that—

LINDA

Was she a sweet soul, Father? Was she exciting?
[*For an instant* EDWARD *loses control of himself.*

EDWARD

Linda, if you are not happy here, why don't you go
away? I should be glad if next month you would take
your maid and Miss Talcott and go on a trip somewhere. You distress me. You cause nothing but trouble and upsets. You—

LINDA

All right, Father. That's just what I'm going to do,
after the wedding. No maid and no Miss Talcott,
though. Just me—Linda—the kid herself—

EDWARD

As you wish.

LINDA

I've wanted to get out for years. I've never known it
so well as to-night. I can't bear it here any longer.
It's doing terrible things to me.

EDWARD

—And will you leave this room now, please?

LINDA

This room—this room—I don't think you'll be able
to stand it long. I'll come back when you've left it—
[*She goes out. There is a silence. Then:*

JULIA

She's dreadful to-night. She's made one situation
after another.

EDWARD

Never mind, my dear. Things will settle themselves. (*He seats himself in a chair at Right.*) Well, Johnny —I don't think I need worry about the way *you'll* take care of Julia, need I?
[JOHNNY *laughs, uncertainly.*

JOHNNY

We'll try to manage!

EDWARD

I consider what you've done, a fine piece of work. I congratulate you.

JULIA

Oh and so do I—so do *I*, dear!
[*She sits near her father.*

JOHNNY

—But you don't know yet, do you?

EDWARD

The fact is, Seton has just now told us.

JULIA

Isn't it marvelous?—Oh what a New Year!

EDWARD

—Your stock is going up with a rush, it seems. It's time to make hay, I think.

JOHNNY

Hay?

EDWARD (*with relish*)

Money! Money!

JULIA

Now all those years you worked so hard—they'll pay interest now, Johnny!

[*The frown grows between* JOHNNY'S *eyes.*

EDWARD

Of course, I could put you into the Bank to-morrow —but I am not sure that that would be advisable at present.

JULIA

—That will come, won't it, Johnny? (*To* EDWARD.) You'd better not wait *too* long, though—he may cost you too much!

[EDWARD *smiles.*

EDWARD

We'll have to risk that. People always do. (*Then seriously.*) Pritchard, Ames is an excellent house. In my opinion, you could not do better than to go with them. Then, in five or six years, you come to us on your own merit. After that, as the children put it, "the sky's the limit." You're in a fair way to be a man of means at forty-five. I'm proud of you.

[*There is a pause. Finally:*

JOHNNY

But—I'd made up my mind not to take the Pritchard, Ames offer.

EDWARD

What? And why not?

JOHNNY

I don't want to get tied-up for life quite so soon. You

see, I'm a kind of a queer duck, in a way. I'm afraid I'm not as anxious as I might be for the things most people work toward. I don't *want* too much money.

EDWARD

Too *much* money?

JOHNNY

Well, more than I need to live by. (*He seats himself facing them and begins eagerly, hopefully, to tell them his plan:*) —You see, it's always been my plan to make a few thousands early in the game, if I could, and then quit for as long as they last, and try to find out who I am and what I am and what goes on and what about it—now, while I'm young, and feel good all the time.—I'm sure Julia understands what I'm getting at—don't you, Julia?
[JULIA *laughs, uncertainly.*

JULIA

I'm not sure I do, Johnny!

EDWARD

You wish to occupy yourself otherwise, is that it?— with some—er—art or other, say—

JOHNNY

Oh no, I've got no abilities that way. I'm not one of the frail ones with a longing to get away from it all and indulge a few tastes, either. I haven't any tastes. Old china and first editions and gate-legged tables don't do a thing to me. I don't want to live any way or in any time but my own—now—in New York— and Detroit—and Chicago—and Phoenix—any place here—but I do want to live!

EDWARD

—As a gentleman of leisure.

JOHNNY

—As a man whose time, for awhile at least, is his own. That's what I've been plugging for ever since I was ten. Please don't make me feel guilty about it, sir. Whether I'm right or wrong, it's more important to me than anything in the world but Julia. Even if it turns out to be just one of those fool ideas that people dream about and then go flat on—even if I find I've had enough of it in three months, still I want it. I've got a feeling that if I let this chance go by, there'll never be another for me. So I don't think anyone will mind if I—just have a go at it—will they, Julia? (JULIA *is silent*.) —Will they, dear?
[JULIA *rises*. JOHNNY *rises with her*.

JULIA (*after a moment*)

Father—will you let Johnny and me talk awhile?

EDWARD

Just a moment— (*He rises and turns to* JOHNNY.) —As I understand it, you have some objection, perhaps, to our manner of living—

JOHNNY

Not for you, sir. I haven't the slightest doubt it's all right for you—or that it's the answer for a lot of people. But for me—well, you see I don't *want* to live in what-they-call "a certain way." In the first place I'd be no good at it and besides that, I don't want to be identified with any one class of people. I want to live every which way, among all kinds—and

know them—and understand them—and love them—
that's what I want!—Don't you, Julia?

JULIA

Why, I—. It sounds—

EDWARD

In all my experience, I have never heard such a—

JOHNNY

I want these years now, sir.

JULIA

Father—please— (*He turns to her. Their eyes meet.*)
—It will be all right, I promise you.
[EDWARD *moves toward the door, where he turns once
more to* JOHNNY.

EDWARD

Case, it strikes me that you chose a strange time to
tell us this, a very strange time.

JOHNNY (*puzzled*)

I don't quite—

EDWARD

—In fact, if I had not already sent the announce-
ment to the newspapers—asked a number of our
friends here to-night to—

JULIA

Father!

JOHNNY (*very quietly*)

Oh, I see.

JULIA

Father—please go down. We'll come in a minute. [EDWARD *hesitates an instant, then goes out.* JOHNNY, *still hopeful, turns to* JULIA.

JOHNNY

—Darling, he didn't get what I'm driving at, at all! My plan is—

JULIA

Oh Johnny, Johnny, why did you do it?

JOHNNY

Do what?

JULIA

You knew how all that talk would antagonize him. [*A moment.*

JOHNNY

You think talk is all it was?

JULIA

I think it was less than that! I'm furious with you.

JOHNNY

It wasn't just talk, Julia.

JULIA

Well, if you think you can persuade me that a man of your energy and your ability, possibly *could* quit at thirty for *any* length of time, you're mistaken.

JOHNNY

I'd like a try at it.

JULIA

It's ridiculous—and why you chose to-night of all nights to go on that way to Father—

JOHNNY

Wait a minute, dear: we'd better get clear on this—

JULIA

I'm clear on it now! If you're tired, and need a holiday, we'll have it. We'll take two months instead of one, if you like. We'll—

JOHNNY

That wouldn't settle anything.

JULIA

Johnny, I've known quite a few men who don't work —and of all the footling, unhappy existences—it's inconceivable that you could stand it—it's unthinkable you could!

JOHNNY

—I might do it differently.

JULIA

Differently!
[*A moment. Then:*

JOHNNY

Julia, do you love me?
[*She looks at him swiftly, then looks away.*

JULIA (*lowly*)

You—you have a great time standing me against a wall and throwing knives around me, don't you?
[*In an instant he has taken her in his arms.*

JOHNNY

Oh, sweet—

JULIA (*against his shoulder*)

What do you do things like that for? What's the matter with you, anyway?
[*He stands off and looks at her.*

JOHNNY

Haven't you the remotest idea of what I'm after? (*She looks at him, startled.*) I'm after—all that's in me, all I am. I want to get it out—where I can look at it, know it. That takes time.—Can't you understand that?

JULIA

But you haven't an idea yet of how exciting *business* can be—you're just beginning! Oh Johnny, see it through! You'll love it. I know you will. There's no such thrill in the world as making money. It's the most—what are you staring at?

JOHNNY

Your face.
[*She turns away.*

JULIA

Oh— you won't listen to me—you won't hear me—

JOHNNY

Yes, I will.
[*A pause. Then* JULIA *speaks in another voice:*

JULIA

And you'd expect me to live on—this money you've made, too, would you?

JOHNNY

Why, of course not. You have all you'll ever need for anything you'd want, haven't you?
[*Another pause, then:*

JULIA

—I suppose it doesn't occur to you how badly it would *look* for you to stop now, does it—

JOHNNY

Look? How? (*She does not answer.*) —Oh—you mean there'd be those who'd think I'd married money and called it a day—

JULIA

There would be. There'd be plenty of them.

JOHNNY

—And you'd mind that, would you?

JULIA

Well, I'm not precisely anxious to have it thought of you.

JOHNNY

—Because *I* shouldn't mind it—and I think that lookout's mine. Oh darling, you don't see what I'm aiming at, either—but try a little blind faith for awhile, won't you? Come along with me—

JULIA

Johnny—
[*She reaches for his hand.*

JOHNNY

—The whole way, dear.

JULIA

—Wait till next year—or two years, and we'll think about it again. If it's right, it can be done, then as well as now.—You can do that for me—for us— can't you?

[*A moment. Then he slowly brings her around and looks into her eyes.*

JOHNNY

You think by then I'd have "come around." That's what you think, isn't it?—I'd have "come around"—

JULIA

But surely you can at least see that if—!

[*She stops, as* LINDA *re-enters.*

LINDA

It lacks six minutes of the New Year, if anyone's interested.

[*A moment, then* JULIA *moves toward the door.*

JULIA

Come on, Johnny.

JOHNNY (*to* LINDA)

Where are the others?

LINDA

My pretty new friends? Well, it seems they've ditched me. (*She starts a tune on the music-box.*) —*This* won't make too much noise, do you think?

JOHNNY

How do you mean, Linda?

LINDA

I imagine Peter and Mary got tired of being put through their tricks, and slid out when they could. Nick and Susan left a message upstairs with Delia saying that they had to go after them. I'm supposed to follow, but I don't think I will, somehow.

JULIA

Oh, I *am* sorry.

LINDA

Are you, Julia? That's a help. (*She goes to the supper-table.*) —Anyone care for a few cold-cuts before the fun starts?

JOHNNY

You're not going to stay up here all alone—

LINDA

Why not? I'm just full of resources. I crack all kinds of jokes with myself—and they say the food's good. (*She takes a bite of a sandwich and puts it down again.*) Ugh. Kiki—

JULIA

Linda, this is plain stubbornness, and you know it. [LINDA *wheels about sharply.*

LINDA

Listen, Julia—! (*She stops, and turn away.*) No— that gets you nowhere, does it?

JULIA (*to* JOHNNY)

Are you coming?

JOHNNY

I think I'll wait a moment with Linda, if you don't mind.

JULIA

But I do mind!—Will you come, please?

JOHNNY

—In a moment, Julia.
[JULIA *looks at him. He meets her gaze steadily. She turns and goes out. There is a pause. Then:*

LINDA

You'd better run on down, don't you think?

JOHNNY

Not right away.
[*Another pause.*

LINDA

I'm afraid I don't know how to entertain you. I've done all my stuff.

JOHNNY

I don't need entertaining.
[*Another pause, a very long one.* LINDA *looks uncertainly toward the music-box. Finally:*

LINDA

—You wouldn't care to step into a waltz, Mr. Case?

JOHNNY

I'd love it. (*She extends her arms, he takes her in his, they begin to waltz slowly to the music-box.*) —There's a conspiracy against you and me, child.

LINDA

What's that?

JOHNNY

The Vested Interests—

LINDA

I know.

JOHNNY

—They won't let you have any fun, and they won't give me time to think.

LINDA

I suppose, like the great fathead you are, you told them all your little hopes and dreams.

JOHNNY

Um.

LINDA

—Pretty disappointing?

JOHNNY

Bad enough.

LINDA

Poor boy.

JOHNNY

How about your own evening?

LINDA

Not so good, either.

JOHNNY

Poor girl.

LINDA

But we won't mind, will we?

JOHNNY

Hell no, we won't mind.

LINDA

We'll get there—

JOHNNY

We'll get there!
[*She stops in the dance and looks up at him for a moment, curiously. Then he smiles at her and she smiles back.*

JOHNNY

—Place head, A, against cheek, B, and proceed as before— (*They begin to dance again.*) —Of course they may be right.

LINDA

Don't you believe it!

JOHNNY

They seem—awfully sure.

LINDA

It's your ride still, isn't it? You know where you want to go, don't you?

JOHNNY

Well, I thought I did.

LINDA

So did I.—Pathetic, wasn't it—all my fuss and fury over anything so unimportant as this party.

JOHNNY

Maybe it was important.

LINDA

Well, if it was, I'm not. And I guess that's the answer.

JOHNNY

Not quite.

LINDA

—Me and my little what-do-you-call-it—defense mechanism—so pathetic. Yes, I'm just chock-full of pathos, I am.

JOHNNY

You're a brick, Linda.

LINDA

Oh, shut your silly face— (*Then:*) You're right, you know—there *is* nothing up the fun-alley.

JOHNNY

Fun-alley?

LINDA

I had a nice little seven-word motto for my life, but I guess she don't work—

JOHNNY

What was it?

LINDA

"Not very important—but pretty good entertainment."

JOHNNY

H'm—

LINDA

For "pretty good" read "rotten." (*They dance for a few moments, silently. Then* LINDA *stops.*) There. That's enough. I'm getting excited.

JOHNNY

—What?

LINDA

—It was grand. Thanks. You can go now. (*She has not yet left his arms. Suddenly from outside comes the sound of bells tolling. Her grasp tightens upon his arm.*) Listen!
[*She looks over her shoulder toward the window. Horns begin to be heard from the distance, long-drawn-out, insistent.*

JOHNNY

It's it, all right.
[*Again she turns her face to his.*

LINDA

Happy New Year, Johnny.
[*He bends and kisses her.*

JOHNNY

Happy New Year, dear.
[*For an instant she clings to him, then averts her face.*

LINDA (*in a breath*)

Oh, Johnny, you're so attractive—

JOHNNY (*with difficulty*)

You're—you're all right yourself—
[*There is a dead silence. Then she leaves his arms, turns and smiles to him.*

LINDA

—You can count on Sister Linda.—Run on down now—quick! They'll be waiting.
[JOHNNY *hesitates.*

JOHNNY

Linda—

LINDA

What?

JOHNNY

They've—your father—I've been put in a position that—

LINDA

Do you love Julia, Johnny?
[*He turns away.*

JOHNNY

Of course I do.
[NED *enters silently, another glass in hand. He stands in the shadow at Left, watching them, swaying almost imperceptibly.*

LINDA

—Well, if ever she needed you, she needs you now. Once it's announced she'll go through with it. Then you can help her. I can't do anything any more. I've tried for twenty years. You're all that's left. Go on, Johnny— (*He goes to the door. From downstairs a swelling chorus of male voices begins Auld Lang Syne.*) —And tell those choir-boys for me, that I'll be in Scotland before them.

[JOHNNY *goes out, closing the door after him.* LINDA *stops the music-box, then moves slowly to the window, Right, where she stands silently for a moment, looking out.* NED *is still watching her, immobile. At length she turns to him:*

LINDA

—Just take any place, Ned.
[*He goes to the couch and sits there.*

NED

—Rum party down there, isn't it?

LINDA

A hundred million dollars knocking together never made many sparks that I could see. (*She takes a glass of wine from the table.*) What's it like to get drunk, Ned?

NED

It's—how drunk?

LINDA

Good and drunk.

NED

Grand.
[*She seats herself near the table, facing him.*

LINDA

How is it?

NED

Well, to begin with, it brings you to life.

LINDA

Does it?

NED

Yes.—And after a little while you begin to know all about it. You feel—I don't know—important—

LINDA

That must be good.

NED

It is.—Then pretty soon the game starts.

LINDA

What game?

NED

—That you play with yourself. It's a swell game—there's not a sweller game on this earth, really—
[LINDA *sips her wine.*

LINDA

How does it go?

NED

Well, you think clear as crystal, but every move, every sentence is a problem. That—gets pretty interesting.

LINDA

I see.

NED

Swell game. Most terribly exciting game.

LINDA

You—get beaten, though, don't you?

NED

Sure. But that's good, too. Then you don't mind anything—not anything at all. Then you sleep.
[*She is watching him, fascinated.*

LINDA

How—how long can you keep it up?

NED

A long while. As long as you last.

LINDA

Oh, Ned—that's awful!

NED

Think so?—Other things are worse.

LINDA

But—but where do you end up?

NED

Where does everybody end up? You die.—And that's
all right, too.
[*A pause. Then:*

LINDA

Ned, can you do it on champagne?

NED

Why— (*He stops and looks at her, intently.*)
—What's the matter, Linda?
[*She finishes her glass and sets it down.*

LINDA

Nothing.

NED

I know.

LINDA

Yes?

NED

Johnny.

LINDA

Give me some more wine, Ned.
[NED *rises and goes over to her.*

NED

He's a funny guy, isn't he?

LINDA

Give me some, Ned—
[*He goes to the table, re-fills her glass, returns, and gives it to her.*

NED

—You can tell me about it, dear.
[LINDA *looks up at him. A moment, then:*

LINDA

I love the boy, Neddy.

NED

I thought so.—Hell, isn't it?

LINDA

I guess it will be.
[NED *raises his glass.*

NED

> Here's luck to you—
> [LINDA *stares at her glass.*

LINDA

> I don't want any luck. (NED *moves away from her to the table near the couch. He finishes his drink, leaves it there and sinks down upon the couch.* LINDA *carefully sets her glass of wine, untouched, upon the supper-table, and rises.*) I think what I'd better do, is— (*She moves slowly to the door, and opens it. The song is just finishing. It is applauded.* LINDA *hesitates, at the door.*) Ned—
> [*He does not answer. Suddenly, from downstairs, comes a long roll of drums.* LINDA *stiffens. She starts to close the door, but is held there, her hand upon the knob.* EDWARD's *voice begins to be heard:*

EDWARD

> Ladies and gentlemen—my very good friends: I have the honor to announce to you the engagement of my daughter, Julia, to Mr. John Case—an event which doubles the pleasure I take in wishing you—and them —a most happy and prosperous New Year.
> [*There is prolonged applause and through it, congratulations and laughter. Slowly, she closes the door but still stands with her hand upon it. Finally she speaks, without turning:*

LINDA

> Ned— (*He does not answer.*) Ned—maybe I ought to go down and—I'm not sure I *will* stay up here— do you mind? (*He is silent. She turns and sees him.*)

Ned! (*He is asleep. She goes to him swiftly, speaking
again, in a low voice:*) Ned— (*A moment. Then:*)
Poor lamb. (*She bends and kisses him. She goes to the
doorway, turns off the lights in the Playroom, and
opens the door. A confusion of excited voices is heard
from downstairs. In the lighted hallway* LINDA *turns
to the stairs, raises her head and goes out, calling
above the voices:*) Hello!—Hello everyone!

CURTAIN

ACT THREE

ACT THREE

Scene: The Same as Act One.
Time: Twelve days later. Ten o'clock at night.
The curtains are drawn and the lamps lighted.
Coffee-service is on a small table near the fireplace.
NICK *and* SUSAN *are taking their coffee.* LINDA'S *cup is*
on the table. She stands near the sofa at Left Center,
frowning at NICK.

LINDA

—No?

[NICK *shakes his head.*

NICK

Not possibly.

[*He is behind the sofa at Right, upon which* SUSAN
is seated.

SUSAN

Why should Johnny pick a place like that?

LINDA

Why should he go away at all?

NICK

I'd have done the same thing—I'd have just giv' 'er
a look, I would, and flounced out.

SUSAN

Hush, Nick. This is no time for fooling.

[LINDA *thinks a minute, then head down, eyes on the*

147

floor, she paces across the room and back, and across again. She stops opposite them and turns:

LINDA

—Atlantic City.

SUSAN

You don't go to Atlantic City for six days to think.

NICK

Old Chinese proverb.

LINDA

But where can he be, then?—*Where?*

SUSAN

Don't worry, Linda. I'm sure he's all right.

NICK

Susan and I parted forever at least forty times. (*To* SUSAN.) —Or was it forty-seven?

SUSAN

Of course.—And they haven't even done that. They've just put off the wedding awhile.

LINDA

I know, but— (*She looks away, anxiously.*) Oh lordy, lordy—

NICK

Johnny will come around, Linda. He's up against the old fight between spirit and matter—anyone want to take a hundred on spirit?

LINDA

I will! I'll take two hundred!

NICK

It's a bet, Madam.
[*He looks at his watch.*

SUSAN

Don't forget we have to go back to the house for our bags, Nick.

NICK

There's lots of time. She doesn't sail until midnight. "She"—a boat that size, "she"—the big nance. (*To* LINDA.) —You don't really want to see us off, do you?

LINDA

Oh, yes! But can you stop back for me on your way down?

SUSAN

If you like.

LINDA

I don't want to leave here till the last minute. I keep feeling that something may happen.

SUSAN

Where's Julia now?

LINDA

She went to dine someplace with Father. He won't let her out of his sight—or into mine.

NICK

No wonder Johnny took to the woods.

LINDA (*quickly*)

—The woods?

NICK

—Or wherever he did take to.

LINDA

Now I know!

SUSAN

Yes?

LINDA

It was at Placid they met. It was at Placid they—of course!

[*She goes to the telephone behind the sofa, at Left.*

NICK (*to* SUSAN)

It may be. They say they always return to the scene of the crime.

LINDA

Long distance, please.

SUSAN

—In which case, I suppose Julia wins.

NICK

I don't know. It's pretty cold at Placid. There's nothing for a rapid pulse like a little wet snow up the sleeve.

LINDA

Long distance please—

SUSAN (*to* NICK)

Would you mind telling me how a man like Johnny is attracted to a girl like that, in the first place?

NICK (*to* SUSAN)

You're too young to know, Susan.

LINDA (*at the telephone*)

—Long distance?

SUSAN

I can think of several people who'd be better for Johnny than Julia.

LINDA

I want to speak with Lake Placid, New York—

NICK

I can think of one, anyway.

LINDA

—Placid—the Lake Placid Club.

SUSAN

Do you suppose she's in love with him?

NICK

Suppose? I know. Look at her.

LINDA

"P-l-a-c-i-d"—

NICK

Tiger, Tiger, Tiger.

LINDA

Quiet a minute, will you? (*To the telephone:*) —

Placid—calm—peaceful. Yes. And I'd like to speak with Mr. John Case.

SUSAN

If I could grab you the way I did, she can—

NICK

But there's more in this than meets the ear, darling —Julia.

LINDA

Quiet! (*Then, to the telephone.*) —Miss Seton. *Linda* Seton. (*To* SUSAN.) —I don't want to give him heart-failure, thinking it's— (*To the telephone.*) —John Case—Lake Placid Club—Linda Seton. Thanks. (*She replaces the receiver and returns to* NICK *and* SUSAN.) I'm sure he's there. I feel it in my bones. [*A pause. Then:*

NICK

Linda, Johnny asked me not to tell anyone, but I think you ought to know something: the fact is, he's got a single cabin on the *Paris* for himself to-night.

LINDA

He—? How do you know?

NICK

Because I got it for him.

LINDA

You don't seriously think he'd do it?

NICK

No—I can't say I do.

LINDA

Well, *I* do! Oh, Lord—then he's in New York now!

NICK

Maybe so.

LINDA

He can't be, or he'd be here.—Where did he go to, Nick?

NICK

—Of that, I wasn't informed.

LINDA

You know, this is ageing me.

SUSAN

We know something else you don't know, Linda.

LINDA

Oh? What is it?

NICK

—Look out, Susan. Steady, girl.

[LINDA *glances at them quickly, then lights a ciga-rette.*

LINDA

What is it?

SUSAN

How did you happen to decide not to come abroad, as you planned?

LINDA

Why I—well, I thought probably Johnny and Julia —they'd rather not have any family tagging along,

and besides that, I want to get Ned off on a trip with
me—out west, if I can.

SUSAN

I know. But—
(*Again* NICK *cuts across her.*

NICK

—I saw Ned in Jimmy's last night. He was—well, if
I may use the word—

SUSAN

Look here, Linda—

LINDA (*to* NICK)

—I think he's all right to-night. He went to a show
with the Wheelers.
[NICK *reflects:*

NICK

I wonder if they're really in love with each other.

LINDA

They're terribly in love.

SUSAN

What makes you think so?

LINDA

I know it. Johnny couldn't help but be, and Julia—
[SUSAN *glances at* NICK.

SUSAN

You meant the Wheelers, didn't you?

NICK

Why, I—yes, I did.

LINDA

I don't know about them.
[*She moves away from them, then back again.*

SUSAN

Can't *you* do anything with her, Linda?

LINDA

Who—Julia?

SUSAN

Yes.

LINDA

I've talked myself blue in the face. It's no good. She
won't listen. I've had the cold-shoulder and the deaf-
ear so long now I'm all hoarse and half-frozen.

SUSAN

I thought she's always depended on you.

LINDA

Well, she doesn't any more.

SUSAN

You love her a great deal, don't you?
[LINDA *laughs shortly.*

LINDA

I expect I do!

SUSAN

—But my dear child, don't you see that if she thinks
just as your father does—

LINDA

Johnny'll fix that. Johnny'll fix everything.

SUSAN

He'll never change *them*, Linda.

LINDA

Susan, you don't know that man.

NICK

—It'd be a pity to deprive your father of the pleasure he'd take in putting him over on the town.

LINDA

Don't speak of it. That's one thing Johnny's been spared so far. I don't think he's had an inkling of *it* yet.

NICK

It will come: Mr. and Mrs. John Sebastian Case have closed their Sixty-fourth Street house and gone to Coney Island for the hunting. Mrs. Case will be remembered as Julia Seton, of Seton Pretty.

SUSAN

I'd like a picture of him, when it happens.

NICK

I wouldn't.

LINDA

—If they'd only listen to me—I've got to make them listen! —And he's so sweet, he's so attractive. What's the matter with the girl, anyway? She ought to know by now that men like Johnny don't grow on every bush.

SUSAN

—But you see, the things you like in him are just

what she can't stand, Linda. And the fate you say
he'll save her from, is the one fate in this whole world
she wants.

LINDA

I don't believe it.—Even so, she loves him—and
there's been a break—and wouldn't you think she'd
at least be woman enough to hang on—*hang on!*

SUSAN

I don't know. There's another who isn't woman
enough to grab.
[*There is a silence. Finally* LINDA *speaks:*

LINDA

—I don't quite get you, Susan.

SUSAN

Well, to make it plain, no man's lost this side of the
altar.

NICK

She's talking a lot of— (*Then, to* SUSAN:) Come on,
Pearl—ups-a-daisy.

LINDA

Susan—

SUSAN

Yes, dear?

LINDA

Julia has never in her life loved anyone but Johnny.

SUSAN

—And you.

LINDA

—And me.

NICK (*in spite of himself*)
—And herself.
[LINDA *turns on him sharply.*

LINDA

That's not true!—Even in this, it's of him she's thinking—she may be mistaken, but it *is* of him!

SUSAN

I've no doubt she believes that.

LINDA

Well, I believe it too!

NICK

—Come on, will you, Susan?

LINDA

I think it's rotten of you to suspect things of Julia that aren't Julia at all, and I think it's worse of you, to—

NICK

We're sorry, Linda, really we are.

LINDA

You aren't sorry! You're— (*Suddenly she covers her face with her hands.*) Oh, what's the matter with me?

SUSAN

Linda, I could shake you.

LINDA

I wish you would.—I wish someone would, till there was nothing left to shake.

SUSAN

—And there's not a thing to do about it?

LINDA

What there is to do, I'm doing.
[*She goes to the window at Back. A silence. Then:*

SUSAN

—And if you did anything else, I expect you wouldn't be Linda.

NICK

Linda, I think you're just about the— (*But that is as close as he can get to a declaration of faith.*) —Oh hell— (*He turns to* SUSAN.) Will you come, dear? It's ten-thirty.
[SUSAN *rises and moves toward* LINDA. NICK *follows.*

SUSAN

But if Johnny should— (LINDA *faces her.*) —Promise us one thing, Linda.

LINDA

What?

SUSAN (*after a moment*)

Nothing.

LINDA

I love you two.

SUSAN

—And so do we love you.

LINDA

—Call back for me when?

SUSAN

In half an hour.

NICK

Less.

LINDA

—Then could your car possibly take me out to Mary Hedges'?

SUSAN

But of course! What a good idea—

LINDA

Mary asked if— I'll have a bag packed. (JULIA *comes in.*) Oh hello, dear.—Are you back already?

JULIA

Isn't it late? Hello, Susan. Hello, Nick. I thought you were sailing.
[*She leaves her evening-wrap on the sofa, Left, and moves toward the writing-table at Right.*

SUSAN

We are.

NICK

At the crack of twelve. On the way now, in fact.

JULIA

I hope you have a grand trip.

SUSAN

Thanks.

[DELIA *enters and takes* JULIA's *wrap from the sofa.*

LINDA

—Delia, will you pack a bag for me, please? I'm going to Mrs. Hedges until Tuesday.

DELIA

Yes, Miss.
[*She goes out.* NICK *and* SUSAN *stand at Center, facing* JULIA.

SUSAN

I'm sorry we won't be here for the wedding, Julia.

JULIA

I'm sorry too, Susan.

NICK

When's it to be?

JULIA

We haven't quite—set a date, yet.

SUSAN

—In the Spring, sometime?

JULIA

Possibly before.

NICK

Let us know, won't you?

JULIA

Of course.
[*A brief pause. Then:*

NICK

—Then you're not coming down to the boat to-night?

JULIA

I'm afraid I can't. Bon voyage, though.
[NICK *thinks rapidly.*

NICK

Thanks. Can we take any word to Johnny for you?

JULIA

To Johnny?

NICK

Yes.—Or a basket of fruit, maybe?

JULIA

He'll be there, will he?
[*This, at any rate,* NICK *can do:*

NICK

I should imagine so, if he's sailing.

JULIA

Sailing!

NICK

Isn't he?

JULIA

I wasn't aware of it.

NICK

Well, all I know is that the morning he left for where-
ever he went to, he telephoned me to get him a single
cabin through Andrews, of the French Line. I don't
believe it's been given up, or I'd have heard from
them. I thought of course you knew, or I—

JULIA

I think I should—if he were going.

NICK

Yes, I suppose so. (*To* SUSAN.) We won't expect him then.

SUSAN

No.—Good-bye, Julia.
[*They move together toward the door.*

NICK

Look us up, when you arrive. Immigrant's Bank. —We'll see you later, Linda.

LINDA

I'll be ready.

SUSAN

Thanks. Lovely evening—

NICK AND SUSAN (*together*)

—And you must come and see *us* sometime!
[*They go out. There is a silence.* JULIA *looks for a cigarette.*

LINDA

It may be true, Julia. I think the chances are it is.

JULIA

What?

LINDA

—That Johnny's going with them.
[JULIA *laughs.*

JULIA

Not possibly, darling!—Why don't they keep these cigarette-boxes filled—

LINDA

Stop it, Julia!

JULIA

Stop it?

LINDA

—Pretending you don't give a damn.
[JULIA *finds and lights a cigarette.*

JULIA

You seem to be taking my little difficulty more seriously than I am.
[*She moves toward the sofa at Left.*

LINDA

If you don't want Johnny to go off to-night and make a hash of both your lives, you'd better send him some word to the boat.
[JULIA *smiles.*

JULIA

Somehow, I don't think that's necessary.

LINDA

Why not?

JULIA

Well, for one reason, because he won't be there. He's no more sailing to-night than I am.

LINDA

You don't know that he's not!

JULIA

I don't know that he is, so I think I'm safe in assuming it.—Do you want to go to the Todds' dinner on Wednesday? They telephoned—

LINDA

—Julia, why do you want to shut me out in the cold like this?

JULIA

I wasn't aware that I was.

LINDA

—But won't you just *talk* to me! Oh please, Julia—

JULIA

I don't know what there is to say.

LINDA

Never so long as I remember has there been anything we couldn't—

JULIA

If there's been any shutting out done, it's you who've done it, Linda.

LINDA

Me? !

JULIA

Johnny and I have had a difference of opinion, and you're siding with him, aren't you?

LINDA

But he's right! He's right for you as well as for himself—

JULIA

I think that's for me to decide.

LINDA

Not Father?

JULIA

Father has nothing to do with it—

LINDA

Oh no!

JULIA

He happens to agree with me where you don't, that's all.

LINDA

We've always agreed before—always.

JULIA

No—I think quite often I've given in, in order to avoid scenes and upsets and—oh, well—
[*A silence. Then:*

LINDA

—Is that true, Julia?

JULIA

You've always been the "stronger character" haven't you? At least people have always thought so. You've made all the decisions, you've always had the ideas—

LINDA

—And you've been resenting me right from the very— (*She moves away from her, toward the fireplace.*) Oh—I can't believe it—

JULIA

It's nothing to get in a state about—and I didn't say I resented you. You've been an immense help,

often. But when it comes to determining my future,
and the future of the man I'm going to marry—
[LINDA *turns on her sharply.*

LINDA

—Your future! What do you want, Julia—just
security? Sit back in your feather-boa among the
Worthies of the World?

JULIA

Well, I'm certain that one thing I *don't* want, is to
start this endless, aimless discussion all over again.

LINDA

But I tell you, you can't *stand* this sort of life forever—not if you're the person I think you are.
And when it starts going thin on you, what'll you
have to hold on to?—Lois Evans shot herself—why?
Franny Grant's up the Hudson in a Sanitarium—
why?

JULIA

I'm sure I don't know.

LINDA

—Nothing left to do or have or want—that's why—
and no insides! There's not a poor girl in town who
isn't happier than we are—at least they still *want*
what we've got—*they* think it's good. (S*he turns
away.*) —If they knew!

JULIA

—And *I* think it's good.

LINDA

Lord, Julia, don't tell me that you *want* it!

JULIA

I want it, and it's all I want.
[*There is a silence. Then:*

LINDA

—Then it's good-bye Julia.

JULIA

Oh Linda, for heaven's sake don't be so ridiculous!
If you're so damn set on being violent, get a few
Russians in and talk life with a great big L to them.
[EDWARD *comes in, an admonishing finger raised.*

EDWARD

Ah—ah—ah!
[LINDA *turns to him.*

LINDA

—Father, I think you're both giving Johnny the rot-
tenest kind of a deal.

EDWARD

In what way?

LINDA

Every way! Why do you do it? It can't be that you
think he's out to marry for money. You must realize
how simple it would have been for him—to conform to
specifications now, and then just not get up some
fine morning.
[EDWARD *moves to the table behind the sofa at Right.*

EDWARD

I don't regard the young man as a fortune-hunter,
Linda.

LINDA

Well, what is it then?

[EDWARD *finds a cigarette and comes forward with it.*

EDWARD

—I think his outlook has merely become—somewhat confused, shall we say, and—

LINDA

—And you'll straighten it out for him.

EDWARD (*to* JULIA)

We shall try, shan't we, daughter?

LINDA

Why hasn't he a right to spend some part of his life as he wants to? He can afford it. What's he got to do? Pile up so much that he can be comfortable on the income of his income?

[EDWARD *seats himself in a chair near the sofa.*)

EDWARD

—That would be an excellent aim, but I think we shall hardly require it of him.

LINDA

I'd like to hear the requirements.

EDWARD

Any self-respecting young man wishes to earn enough to support his wife and his family.

LINDA

Even when his wife already has——? Even when there's no possible need of it?

EDWARD

Even then.

LINDA

Oh Father, what a fake idea that is!

EDWARD

I don't think so. Nor does Julia.—In addition, he has somehow developed a very curious attitude toward work—

LINDA

It seems to me saner than most. He wants his leisure at this end—good sense, I call it.— Which is harder to do, anyway—? Go to an office and rustle papers about, or sit under a tree and look at your own soul?

JULIA (*contemptuously*)

Heavens!—The office, I should say.

LINDA

Then you've never looked, Julia.

JULIA

You can't talk to her, Father.

EDWARD

I should like to understand what he—and you—are aiming at, Linda, but I must confess I cannot. (NED *comes in.*) —I consider his whole attitude deliberately un-American.

[LINDA *stares at* EDWARD.

LINDA

Are you serious?

EDWARD

Entirely.

[*She stares for a moment more.*)

LINDA

—You're right. I believe it is.

[NED *seats himself on the sofa, at Left.*

NED

I've always said the Americans were a great little people.

LINDA

—Then he's a bad one, and will go to hell when he dies. Because apparently he can't quite believe that a life devoted to piling up money is all it's cracked up to be.—That's strange, isn't it—when he has us, right before his eyes, for such a shining example.

JULIA

I thought *you* were the one who found leisure so empty.

LINDA

—You think I call this, leisure? A life-sentence to *this?*—Or that he does?

JULIA

I think any variety of it he'd find quite as empty.

LINDA

—Even if it should be, he's got a right to discover it for himself! Can't you see that?

JULIA

I can see the discovery would come, quick enough.

LINDA

—And you don't want to be with him to lend a hand, if it should?
[JULIA *is silent.*

EDWARD

Linda, I listened most attentively to our young dreamer the other day. I have listened quite as attentively to you this evening. I am not entirely without intelligence, but I must still confess that most of your talk seems to me to be of the seventeen-year-old variety.

LINDA

I'm glad, if it is! We're all grand at seventeen. It's after that that the—sickness sets in.
[EDWARD *chuckles, shakes his head and rises.*

EDWARD

—I feel very well, myself—and you look in perfect health, my dear.
[*He moves toward the door.*

LINDA

—You both think he'll come around, Father—compromise, anyway. You'll get fooled. He won't give way one little inch.
[*At the door* EDWARD *turns, smiling.*

EDWARD

Stubborn—?

LINDA

Right! And sure he's right!

EDWARD

We shall see—
[*He goes out, victor.*

JULIA

—Is that all, Linda?

LINDA

Where are you going?

JULIA

To bed.

LINDA

Now?

JULIA

Yes. Have you any objections?

LINDA

You actually won't lift a finger to keep him off that boat to-night?

JULIA

He has no idea of taking it.

LINDA

You don't know him!

JULIA

Well, I think I know him a little better than you. I happen to be engaged to him.
[HENRY *has entered with a tray containing a decanter of whisky, ice, a bottle of soda, and one glass.*

NED

Thanks, Henry.
[HENRY *bows and goes out.*

JULIA

Ned, I thought you went to the theatre with the Wheelers—

NED

I did, but it was so bad I left.
[*He rises, goes behind the table and makes himself a drink.*

JULIA

Wasn't that just a trifle rude?

NED

I don't know, Julia. Look it up under R in the book of Etiquette, will you?

JULIA

I can't imagine what you're thinking of these days.— Drinking alone—that's pretty too, isn't it?

NED

I never thought of the aesthetic side, but I see what you mean.
[*He takes a long swallow of his drink.* JULIA *regards him contemptuously, then:*

JULIA (*to* LINDA)

If there's any message of any sort, I wish you'd ring my room.

LINDA

All right.

[JULIA *goes out.* LINDA *seats herself and stares mood-
ily in front of her.*

NED

—Like a drink?

LINDA

No thanks.
[NED *again settles down upon the sofa.*

NED

—You know, most people, including Johnny and
yourself, make a big mistake about Julia.

LINDA

What's that?

NED

They're taken in by her looks. At bottom she's a
very dull girl, and the life she pictures for herself
is the life she belongs in.
[*The telephone rings.* LINDA *goes to it.*

LINDA

—You've never hit it off, that's all. (*At the telephone.*) Hello.—Yes.—Yes.—What? When, do you
know?—Well ask, will you? (*To* NED.) He *was* there.

NED

Who and where?

LINDA

Johnny—Placid. (*To the telephone.*) Yes? This—?
I see. No. No. That's right. Thanks. (*She puts down
the telephone and turns again to* NED.) —And left
this noon.

NED

Then he'll be around to-night.

LINDA

You think so? This late?

NED

He'll be around.
[*A moment. Then:*

LINDA

Ned—

NED

What?

LINDA

Do you remember what we talked about New Year's
Eve?
[*A brief pause. Then:*

NED

Sure—I remember.

LINDA

Tell me something—

NED

Sure.

LINDA

Does it stand out all over me?

NED

Why?

LINDA

Nick and Susan—I think they got it.

NED

Anyone who loves you would, Linda.

LINDA

Oh, that's awful. I'm so ashamed— (*Then she raises her head.*) I'm not, though!

NED

Why should you be?

LINDA (*suddenly*)

Look here, Ned—you're in a jam too, aren't you?

NED

Me?

LINDA

You.

NED

Sure, I suppose so.

LINDA

Is it that you hate this— (*Her gesture includes the house and all it represents.*) —Or that you love that—

[*She indicates his drink.*

NED

H'm— (*He looks about him.*) Well, God knows I hate all this— (*And lifts the glass before his eyes.*) —And God knows I'm crazy mad over this— (*He takes a deep swallow and sets the glass down.*) I guess it's both.

LINDA

What are we going to do?

NED

Nothing, that I know of.

LINDA

But we must!
[NED *hunches down into the sofa.*

NED

I'm all right.

LINDA

You're not—but you'll pull out of it—and *I'll* pull out of it.

NED

I'm all right. I don't mind any more.

LINDA

You've got to mind. We can't just let go, can we?

NED

I can. I have.

LINDA

No. No!

NED

Listen, Linda: I've had the whole thing out with myself, see? All of it. A lot of times. And I've developed my what-do-you-call-it—technique. I'm all right. There's no reason for stewing over me. I'm— (*He squints at his glass.*)—very happy.

LINDA

There must be some sort of life for you—

NED

—But there *is!* Haven't I got the swell Seton name to uphold? (*He laughs shortly.*) —Only that's where I'll fox it. I'll make *it* uphold me.

LINDA

Neddy—listen: After the wedding we'll go out to Boulder, both of us.— We'll live on horseback and in trout streams all day long every day until we're in hand again. We'll get so damn tired that we won't be able to want anything or think of anything but sleep.

NED

You make it too hard. Come on—have a drink—

LINDA

Oh, you're dying, Neddy!

NED (*very patiently*)

All right, Linda.

LINDA

Won't you do that with me?

NED

Thanks, but uh-uh. Nope.
[LINDA *moves away from him to the other side of the room.*

LINDA

Oh, won't anyone ever again do what I *know* they should do?

NED

That's what's the matter with you, Linda. You

worry so much over other people's troubles, you
don't get anywhere with your own.

[HENRY *enters.* LINDA *is staring at* NED.

HENRY

—Mr. Case, Miss.

[*A silence, then* LINDA *recovers herself.*

LINDA

Yes?— Have him come up, will you?

[HENRY *bows and goes out. A moment.* NED *watches her. Then:*

NED

—Are you sure you *want* to get over him?

LINDA

No. I'm not. And that's what scares me most. I feel
alive, and I love it. I feel at last something's hap-
pening to me. But it can't get anywhere, so it's like
living on—*your* stuff. I've *got* to get over it.

NED

—Because it seems so hopeless, is that it?

LINDA

Seems! What do you mean?

NED

Don't you know? (LINDA *can only look at him. He
goes to her.*) —Then let me tell you something:
you're twice as attractive as Julia ever thought of
being. You've got twice the looks, and twice the mind,
and ten times the guts. You've lived in her shade for
years, now, and there's nothing to it. You could
charm a bird off a tree, if you would. And why not?

If you were in her way, she'd ride you down like a rabbit.

LINDA (*softly*)

Oh you stinker—knowing the way she loves him—you stinker, Ned.
[NED *shrugs*.

NED

All right. (*He wanders in the direction of the door.*) —Tell him Hello for me, will you?
[LINDA'S *voice rises:*

LINDA

—If there's one thing I'll do in my life, it'll be to let the fresh air back into you again, hear me?—I'll do it if I have to shoot you.
[NED *turns and smiles back at her.*

NED

—All right.
[*He goes out. With an exclamation* LINDA *goes to the window and looks out, huddling herself in her arms.* JOHNNY *enters. A moment, then:*

JOHNNY

Hello, Linda.

LINDA

Hello, Johnny.

JOHNNY

Is—?
[LINDA *moves to the telephone.*

LINDA

I'll send for her.

JOHNNY

Wait a minute. (*A silence. He looks about him.*) I feel as if I'd—been away quite awhile.

LINDA

Yes.

JOHNNY

I went to Placid.

LINDA

I see.

JOHNNY

It was horrible there.

LINDA

I can imagine it.

JOHNNY

Oh Linda, I love her so—

LINDA

Of course you do, Johnny.

JOHNNY

It—makes anything else—any plans—ideas—anything—

LINDA

—Seem so unimportant, of course.

JOHNNY

But I know they are important! I know that!
[LINDA *smiles.*

LINDA

Still—
[JOHNNY *turns away.*

JOHNNY

That's it—*still*—
[*A moment.*

LINDA

I think it'll come out all right, Johnny.

JOHNNY

Maybe, in the long run.

LINDA

Have you—I suppose you've decided something or
other—

JOHNNY

I'm going to stay at my job, if that's what you
mean.

LINDA (*After a moment, very quietly:*)

I see.

JOHNNY

But only for awhile! Only a couple of years, say—
just until I can get through to her that—well, it's
what she asked, and after all, a couple of years isn't
a lifetime.

LINDA

No, of course not.

JOHNNY

I can see the way they look at it—I could hardly expect them suddenly to do a complete about-face, and—but hang it, they ought at least to see what I'm getting at!

LINDA

Perhaps eventually they will.

JOHNNY

That's what I'm counting on.
(*Another silence. Then:*

LINDA

The fun's gone out of you, Johnny. That's too bad.
[JOHNNY *stares at the floor.*

JOHNNY

It'll be back.

LINDA

I hope.
[JOHNNY *looks up suddenly.*

JOHNNY

Linda—you agree that there's only the one thing for me to do now—
[LINDA *smiles again.*

LINDA

Compromise—

JOHNNY

Yes, damn it! But *you* think that's right, don't you?

LINDA

I don't think it matters a bit what I think—
[JOHNNY *goes to her suddenly and seizes her wrists.*

JOHNNY

It does, though! You think it's right, don't you?
Say you think it's right!

LINDA

Shall I send for Julia?

JOHNNY

Say it first!

LINDA (*with difficulty*)

Johnny—when two people love each other as much
as you, anything that keeps them apart must be
wrong.—Will that do? (JOHNNY *drops her hand and
moves away from her.*) —And shall I send for her
now?

JOHNNY

Go ahead.
LINDA *goes to the telephone and presses a button in
the box beside it.*

LINDA

With luck, we'll manage not to include Father this
time.

JOHNNY

Oh Lord, yes! (LINDA *again presses the button, and
again several times.*) Asleep, probably—

LINDA

Of course not. (*She presses it again. Then:*) Julia—

yes—would you come down a minute? No—but there's no telegram *to* send up. Will you come, Julia? (*Her voices changes.*) Julia, it's terribly important that you come down here at once. (*She replaces the telephone and turns to* JOHNNY.) She'll be right down.

JOHNNY

If she doesn't fall asleep again.

LINDA

Johnny—don't talk like that. I can't stand to hear your voice do that.

JOHNNY

You care more what happens to me than she does.

LINDA (*startled*)

What? Don't be silly. (*Then, with difficulty:*) —Maybe I feel things about you that she doesn't because—well, maybe just because *I'm* not in love with you.

JOHNNY

You know what I think of you, don't you?
[LINDA *smiles.*

LINDA

I'd be glad to hear.

JOHNNY

I like you better than anyone else in the world.

LINDA

That's very nice, Johnny—because I like you a good deal, too. (*For a long moment their eyes hold them*

together. Then EDWARD *comes in and, with a start,*
LINDA *sees him.*) Oh, for the love of Pete—
[EDWARD *advances to* JOHNNY, *hand outstretched.*

EDWARD

Well, well—good evening!

JOHNNY

Good evening, sir.
[*They shake hands.* LINDA *turns away.*

LINDA

—Both members of this club.

EDWARD

They tell me you've been away. Very pleasant, having you back.

JOHNNY

It's pleasant to be back.

EDWARD

—Quite at the mercy of the snow these days, aren't
we?

JOHNNY

Quite.
[EDWARD *moves toward the fireplace.*

EDWARD

Still, they say Americans need four seasons, so I suppose we oughtn't to complain, eh?

JOHNNY

I suppose not.

LINDA

Father—Johnny came to-night to see Julia—

EDWARD

—That doesn't surprise me a great deal, daughter—
not a great deal!

LINDA

—Julia—not you and me.—Come on—let's go bye-
bye.

[JULIA *enters.*

JULIA

Linda, what's the idea of—? (*She sees* JOHNNY.)
Oh—

[JOHNNY *goes to her swiftly.*

JOHNNY

Get a wrap, will you? We're going out—

[JULIA *hesitates.*

JULIA

Father—you won't mind if Johnny and I—

EDWARD

Please close the door. I wish to speak with both of
you. (JULIA *gestures helplessly to* JOHNNY *and closes
the door.*) —You insist upon putting me in a position that I don't in the least relish— (JULIA *seats
herself upon the bench at Left. The door is opened
again, tentatively.*) Who's that?—Oh, come in, Ned,
come in.

[NED *enters and moves toward his drink.*

NED

Sorry.—I just wanted—

EDWARD

Sit down, son— (NED *seats himself upon the sofa, Left.* EDWARD *continues to* JULIA *and* JOHNNY:) —Coming between two young people in love, is furthest from my wish and intention.—Love, true love, is a very rare and beautiful thing, and— (NED *rises and moves silently toward the door.*) Where are you going? Please sit down! (*He waits until* NED *has returned to his place, then continues.*) —And I believe its path—that is to say, the path of true love, contrary to the adage, *should* run smooth. But in order that it may—I am a man of fifty-eight years, and speak from a long experience and observation— it is of paramount importance that—

JOHNNY

I beg your pardon, sir.

EDWARD

Yes?

JOHNNY

If Pritchard, Ames still want me, I'll go with them when we get back from our wedding-trip—about March first, say.

[LINDA *turns away. There is a silence. Then:*

JULIA (*softly*)

Oh, Johnny—

[*She goes to him.*

JOHNNY

I'm still not convinced—I still don't believe in it, but it's what Julia wishes and—and I'm—glad to defer to her wish.

LINDA

And now, in heaven's name, may they be left alone—
or shall we all move over to Madison Square Gar-
den?

EDWARD (*disregarding her*)

You are not convinced, you say—
[LINDA *exclaims impatiently.*

JOHNNY

Would you like me to lie to you, sir?

JULIA

It's enough for me, Father.

JOHNNY

Julia said a year or two. I'll stay with them three
years. I'll work harder than ever I've worked before. I'll do everything I can to make a success of
it. I only ask that if at the end of the three years I
still feel that it's wise to quit for awhile, there won't
be any more objections.

EDWARD

I doubt if by that time there'll be reason for any.

JOHNNY

We'll have to see about that, sir.

JULIA

Well, Father?
[*A pause. Then:*

EDWARD

When is it you wish to be married?

JULIA

As soon as possible.

JOHNNY

Sooner.

EDWARD

The invitations must be out for ten days at least.—
How would two weeks from Wednesday suit you?

JULIA

That would be perfect.

EDWARD

No doubt there will be a sailing later that week.—
Well now, the sun's shining once more, isn't it?—
And we're all friends again, eh?

LINDA

Just one big family.

EDWARD

—And what are your plans for your wedding-trip,
may I ask?

JOHNNY

We haven't any very definite ones. Mostly France,
I expect.

EDWARD

It's well to arrange even honeymoons a bit in advance.
—Now let me suggest a little itinerary: You'll land
at Plymouth or Southampton, and proceed straight
to London. I'll cable my sister to-morrow. She and
her husband will be delighted to have you stay with
them.

LINDA

Good Lord, Father—

EDWARD (*to* JOHNNY)

He is Sir Horace Porter—one of the most important men in British banking circles.

JULIA

Father, I'm not sure—

EDWARD

You can scarcely go abroad and not stop with your Aunt Helen, Julia. In addition, it will save hotel expense and Johnny will be able to learn something of British methods.—Then I shall cable the Bouviers in Paris.—He was expert adviser to the Minister of Finance in the late war—a very good man for you to know. If they aren't already in Cannes, they will be very glad to have you visit them. And if they are, you could not do better than go straight to the South yourselves and—

JOHNNY

I had thought of this as more of a lark than a business-trip, sir.

EDWARD

—But there's no harm in combining a little business with pleasure, is there? I've never found there was.

JULIA (*to* JOHNNY)

They have a lovely place in Cannes.

EDWARD

A week in London—a week in Paris—

LINDA

An hour in the Louvre—

EDWARD

—Ten days in Cannes—ideal! Then you might sail from Genoa and return by the Southern route. (*To* JULIA.) I'll arrange to have your house ready for you to go into March first.

JULIA

—Thanks, dear.

JOHNNY

What house is that, Julia?

JULIA

Father's lending us the sweetest little place on Sixty-fourth Street.

NED (*to* LINDA)

Would you call the Sixty-fourth Street house little?

LINDA (*watching* JOHNNY)

—By comparison.

EDWARD (*to* JULIA)

And I have also decided to turn the cottage at The Poplars over to you for the summers.

JULIA

Father, you shouldn't—you really should not!
[*She goes to him and takes his hand.*

NED

Now there *is* a small place—hasn't even got a ball-room.

JULIA

Oh Johnny—wait till you see it!
[EDWARD *is beaming.*

EDWARD

This is not a deed of gift, you know—not yet. Perhaps when you have occupied them for—er—five years or so, my hard old heart may soften.

JULIA

—Listen to him—*his* hard old heart! (*To* JOHNNY.) —Have you ever known of anyone so sweet?

JOHNNY (*after a moment*)

Julia—I'm sorry—but I can't stand it.
[*A silence. Then:*

JULIA

Would you—mind telling me what you mean?

JOHNNY

If we begin loaded down with possessions, obligations, responsibilities, how would we ever get out from under them? We never would.

EDWARD

Ah?

JOHNNY

—No. You're extremely generous—and kind—but it's not for me.

EDWARD

And may I ask what *is* for you?

JOHNNY

I don't know yet, but I do know it's not this.

EDWARD (*very quietly*)

We are to understand, then, that you are *not* returning to work.

JOHNNY

That work? For this? (*He shakes his head.*) —No.

JULIA

But you said—!

JOHNNY

—I'm back where I was, now. I can see now that it's got to be a clean break, it's simply got to.

EDWARD

But the other day, if I remember correctly, you intimated that you might follow some occupation—

JOHNNY

Eventually, yes. I think I may still be fairly active at thirty-five or forty.

EDWARD

—And in the meantime you expect just to lie fallow, is that it?

JOHNNY

Not lie—be! I expect to dig and plow and water for for all I'm worth.

EDWARD

Toward the—er—eventual occupation which is to overtake you—

JOHNNY

Exactly.

EDWARD

I see.—Julia, if you marry this young man now, I doubt if he will ever again earn one penny.
[*He moves to the table behind the sofa, at Right.* JOHNNY *advances.*

JOHNNY

Julia, if it's important to you, I'll promise you I shall always earn my own living. And what's more, if there's need of it, I'll always earn yours.

JULIA

Thanks.

JOHNNY

Oh my dear, we've got to make our own life—there's nothing to it, if we don't—there's no other way to live it!—Let's forget wedding-invitations and two weeks from Wednesday. Let's go now. Let's be married to-night.
[EDWARD *turns, in amazement.*

JULIA

I must decide now, must I?

JOHNNY

Please—

JULIA

—And if I say No—not unless you—?

JOHNNY

—Then I'm going to-night, by myself.
[*A moment. Then:*

JULIA

Very well—you can go. Because I don't quite see myself with an idler for a husband.
[*A silence. Then* JOHNNY *speaks, slowly.*

JOHNNY

I suppose the fact is, I love feeling free inside even
better than I love you, Julia.

JULIA

Apparently—or what you call feeling free.
[JOHNNY *turns to* EDWARD.

JOHNNY

Good-bye, sir. I'm sorry we couldn't make a go of
it. Thanks for trying anyhow. (*He goes to* LINDA
and takes both her hands.) —Good-bye to you,
Linda. You've been sweet.

LINDA

Good-bye, Johnny. So have you.—I hope you find
what you're looking for.

JOHNNY

I hope *you* do.

LINDA

You did want someone along with you on the big
search, didn't you?

JOHNNY

I did, you know.

LINDA

Poor boy.

JOHNNY

—But we won't mind, will we?

LINDA

Hell, no—*we* won't mind.

JOHNNY

We'll get there—

LINDA

Sure! *We'll* get there!

JOHNNY

Linda—
[SHE *leans toward him.*

LINDA

Oh please do—
[JOHNNY *bends, kisses her briefly, and moves toward the door.*

JOHNNY

Good-bye, Ned.
[NED *attempts a good-bye, but cannot say it.* JOHNNY *goes out. There is complete silence for a moment. Then* LINDA *murmurs:*

LINDA

I'll miss that man.
[*Another silence, which* JULIA *finally breaks:*

JULIA (*half to herself:*)

—He's really gone, then.

EDWARD

Yes.—And in my opinion—
[LINDA *turns sharply*.

LINDA

—Good riddance, eh?
[EDWARD *nods, sagely*.

JULIA

—Really gone—
[LINDA *goes to her*.

LINDA

—Oh never mind dear, never mind. If he loves you,
he'll be back!
[JULIA *turns upon her*.

JULIA

—Be back? Be *back*, did you say? What do you
think I am? Do you think all I've got to do with my
time is to persuade a—a lightweight like him that
there's something to life but having fun and more
fun?
[LINDA *stares, unable to speak*.

EDWARD

I hope, Julia, that this experience, hard as it may
have been, will teach you that—

JULIA

Oh don't worry about me! I'm all right. (*She laughs
briefly*.) —Even a little more than all right, I
should say.
[NED *rises*.

NED

    —Um.—Narrow squeak, wasn't it?
    [*Suddenly* LINDA *grasps* JULIA's *arm.*

JULIA

    What's the matter with you?

LINDA

    You don't love him.

JULIA

    Will you kindly let go my arm?

LINDA

    You don't love him!

JULIA

    Will you *please*—

LINDA

    Answer me! Do you or do you not?

JULIA

    And what's that to you, may I ask?

EDWARD

    Now children—

LINDA

    What's it to me! Oh, what's it to me! (*Her grasp tightens on* JULIA's *arm.*) Answer me!

JULIA

    Father—what's the matter with her?

LINDA

You don't, do you? I can *see* you don't. It's written all over you. You're relieved he's gone—*relieved!*

JULIA

And suppose I am?

LINDA

—She asks me suppose she is! (*Again she confronts* JULIA.) Are you? Say it!
[JULIA *wrenches herself free.*

JULIA

—I'm so relieved, I could sing with it.—Is that what you want?

LINDA

Yes!—Thanks! (*She throws back her head and laughs with joy, and moves quickly to the table behind the sofa at Left.*) Oh lordy, lordy—have I got a job now!
[*From her handbag on the table she takes two brown envelopes, goes to* NED *and gives him one of them.*

NED

What is it? (*He sees.*) Passport—

LINDA

What do you say?

NED

When?

LINDA

Now. To-night.

NED

Oh, I couldn't, to-night.

LINDA

Of course you could! If I can, you can.
[EDWARD *advances*.

EDWARD

Linda, where are you off to?

LINDA (*to* NED)

Will you come?

NED

Well you know I'd like to, but—

LINDA

Then come!

EDWARD

Linda, where are you going? Tell me instantly.

LINDA

—On a trip. On a big ride. Oh, what a ride! Do you
mind?

NED

Listen, Father: I'd—

EDWARD

A trip now is out of the question. Please remember
you have a position to fill. You are not an idler. (*To*
LINDA.) —A trip where?

LINDA (*to* NED)

You won't?

NED

> I can't.

LINDA

> —Caught.

NED

> Maybe.

LINDA

> —I'll be back for you, Ned.

NED (*almost inaudibly*)

> I'll—be here—
>
> [DELIA *enters.*

DELIA

> Excuse me, Miss Linda—Mr. and Mrs. Potter are waiting in the car. Your bag has gone down.

LINDA

> Bring my fur coat, will you, Delia?—And throw a couple of hats in the hat-box and take it down, too.

DELIA

> Very well, Miss.
>
> [DELIA *goes out.* LINDA *turns to* JULIA.

LINDA

> —You've got no faith in Johnny, have you Julia? His little dream may fall flat, you think—yes! So it may! What about it? What if it should? There'll be another—the point is, he *does* dream! Oh, I've got all the faith in the world in Johnny. Whatever he does is all right with me. If he wants to sit on his tail, he can sit on his tail. If he wants to come back

and sell peanuts, Lord how I'll believe in those peanuts!—Good-bye, Julia. —Good-bye, Father. (*She leaves them and goes to* NED.) Good-bye, Neddy—

NED

Good-bye, kid—good luck—
[*For a moment they cling together. Then:*

LINDA

Oh never you fear, I'll be back for you, my fine bucko!

NED

All right, kid.
[*She moves toward the door.* NED *is drawn after her.* DELIA *enters with the fur coat.* LINDA *takes it from her.* DELIA *goes out.*

EDWARD

As yet you have not said where it is you are—
[JULIA *exclaims suddenly:*

JULIA

I know!

LINDA (*going out*)

—And try to stop me, someone! Oh please—someone try to stop me!
[*She is gone.* NED *stands looking after her, murmuring softly:*

NED

Oh God, oh God—

EDWARD

I shall not permit it! I shall—

NED

—Permit it!—Permit Linda?—Don't make me laugh, Father.

JULIA (*advancing*)

She's going *with* them, isn't she? *Isn't* she?
[NED *smiles and picks up his glass again.*

NED

—Going to get her Johnny.
[JULIA *laughs shortly.*

JULIA

A fine chance she's got!

NED

—Any bets? (*Then savagely:*) —Any bets, Julia? (*He raises his glass.*) —To Linda— (*The portrait above the fireplace catches his eye:*) —And while we're at it—Grandfather!
[*He drinks.*

CURTAIN